# DOC BAR

## By Gala Nettles

Photo by David Brown
Doc Bar at age 21, taken March of 1977 at the Doc Bar Ranch in Paicines, California.

Copyright Gaia Nettles, 1995
All rights reserved

Printed in the United States of America by
PrintComm, Inc.
1451 Empire Central, Suite 106
Dallas, Texas 75247
(214) 630-6601

ISBN 0-9649288-0-9

Typeset by Pro Publishing
Rte 2, Box 118
Boyd, Texas 76023
(817) 433-5232

Cover design by:
PrintComm, Inc.

Without limiting the rights under copyright reserved above, no part of this book may be reproduced, stored in or introduced into a retrieval system, or transmitted, in any form or by any means (electronic, mechanical, photocopying, recording or otherwise), without the prior written permission of the copyright owner of this book.


Extra copies may be ordered from:
LMH Publishing Company
Route 2, Box 60
Groesbeck, Texas 77864
1-800-729-2234

# *Dedication*

*To my mother Mondell Helms.
If everyone had a Mother like you, Mom,
what a bright world this would be.*

# Acknowledgements

I could not have accomplished such an undertaking as this book on Doc Bar without an abundance of help from others. In reality, this book belongs to them, the behind-the-scenes people. I only wrote their stories and printed their facts.

I am indebted to Carolyn Crist at the National Cutting Horse Association and Leslie Groves at the <u>Quarter Horse Journal</u>, who patiently hunted statistic after statistic for me; to Jay Pumphrey and Larry Thornton who tried to teach me genetics; to David Brown, Dave Jones, Bill Baldwin, Roger McMahan, Stephenie and Charlie Ward, Thea Essenger, Don Dodge, Duane Pettibone, Jack Brainard, Darryl Lund, Bobby Ingersoll, Keith Christie and a host of others who spent hours telling Doc Bar stories.

I especially thank three dear friends - horseman Jim Fox in California, English teacher Myra Franklin in Madisonville, Texas, Glory Ann Kurtz, editor of the <u>Quarter Horse News</u>, - who proofread again and again to try to keep me from embarrassing myself with grammatical mistakes and misquoted facts.

And to my family, who ate so many sandwiches without complaining, who forfeited the lake house this summer because Mom barricaded herself there to write, who overlooked my grumpy attitude when words wouldn't flow, you're all just as much a champion as Doc Bar!

*- Gala Nettles*

# Table Of Contents

|  | Page |
|---|---|
| *The Prologue* | *1* |
| *Chapter 1 - Blue Blood Pedigrees for the Perfect Birth* | *4* |
| *Chapter 2 - The Racing Years* | *12* |
| *Chapter 3 - Charley Araujo* | *18* |
| *Chapter 4 - Perceiving The Gold* | *27* |
| *Chapter 5 - Poco Tivio* | *33* |
| *Chapter 6 - The Jensens* | *42* |
| *Chapter 7 - The Purchase Of Doc Bar* | *50* |
| *Chapter 8 - Those Great Poco Tivio Daughters* | *59* |
| *Chapter 9 - The Wards* | *65* |
| *Chapter 10 - Fizzabar* | *71* |
| *Chapter 11 - Poco Lena Comes To Doc Bar* | *76* |
| *Chapter 12 - Prime Time* | *86* |
| *Chapter 13 - The Progeny* | *93* |
| *Chapter 14 - Myth Versus Reality* | *103* |
| *Chapter 15 - The Golden Years* | *110* |
| *Chapter 16 - The Cow Palace* | *115* |
| *Chapter 17 - The End* | *121* |

# Preface

*The great horse Doc Bar led a unique life. He was owned by only two owners in his lifetime; that for which he was most famous, he never did; he retained his prominence although he lived far off the beaten path; and from his remote valley he still was able to build a dynasty.*

*Call it serendipity, call it destiny, call it fate. Whatever, Doc Bar, whose life was influenced by three families, has emerged as one of the leading sires of the Quarter Horse Industry.*

*This project was suggested to me several years ago by a gentleman at the American Quarter Horse Association. At that time, I questioned the reader-appeal of the life of a horse that I knew only from statistics. I now know my hesitancy was unwarranted. The life of Doc Bar reminds me of a Fourth of July fireworks. It was beautiful and I'm so glad I didn't miss it.*

*- Gala Nettles*

Horses are a way of life for author Gala Nettles, who is married to cutting horse trainer Ronnie Nettles and lives on the Nettles Cutting Horse Ranch in Madisonville, Texas. As a free-lance writer, she specializes in agricultural and human-interest writing for numerous magazines, including several publications for foreign countries and two newspaper columns.

Doc Bar, while her fifth book, is her first about the life of a horse. Like so many people in the cutting horse business, the great sire touched her life when her husband, Ronnie Nettles, won the 1984 NCHA Futurity on Doc Per, a great grandson of the stallion.

"I've always enjoyed writing," commented Nettles, who has a Bachelor's degree from Baylor University and a Master's degree from Sam Houston State University. "Writing requires time, so you put more of your heart into it than you do the spoken word. Old letters bring some of the fondest memories."

# Forward

*Through all my years as Editor of the Quarter Horse News, no horse has been more influential on the cutting horse of today than Doc Bar. His name turns up more often in the pedigrees of today's great cutting horses, than any other sire.*

*I feel fortunate to have lived during the lifetime of Doc Bar; however, I feel unfortunate that I was never personally able to see him.*

*Gala, however, has brought Doc Bar to life. She has the unique ability to bring you into the scenario with what she is writing about, and I feel now, after reading this book, that I have personally known Doc Bar.*

*I'm grateful that Gala was able to recreate the important times in the life of Doc Bar, bringing the reader into these happenings and introducing them to the people that were responsible for his rise to fame. This made me realize that this was not just statistics or a fairytale horse or fairytale people - they were real, down-to-earth people that made the right decisions to make Doc Bar the legend he is today.*

*This book is a "must read" for anyone at all interested in performance Quarter Horses. This great stallion was the cornerstone that our industry is built on - and Gala has done an outstanding job of telling it like it was.*

*- Glory Ann Kurtz*

*Seeds spring from seeds, Beauty breedth Beauty,*
*By law of Nature thou art bound to Breed,*
*That things may live, where thou thyself art dead;*
*and so, in spite of death thou dost survive,*
*In that thy likeness still is left alive.*

*Anonomyous*

Photo by John H. Williamson

**Doc Bar in his prime**

# DOC BAR
## (1956-1992)

AQHA #76136                                                 Sorrel Stallion

```
                    ┌ Three Bars  ┌ Percentage
    Lightning Bar  ─┤             └ Myrtle Dee
                    └ Della F     ┌ Doc Horn
                                  └ Mare by Old DJ

                    ┌ Texas Dandy ┌ My Texas Dandy
    Dandy Doll     ─┤             └ Streak
                    └ Bar Maid    ┌ Bartender II
                                  └ Nelly Bly
```

**Breeder:** Finley Ranches, Gilbert, Arizona
**Recorded Owner:** Dr. and Mrs. Stephen F. Jensen, Orinda, California

### AQHA Performance Record:

4 race starts, 0 wins                                        36 halter points

### Sire AQHA Summary:

485 foals from 19 crops
275 performers:

| | | | |
|---|---|---|---|
| Race: | 7 starters | Show: | 308 Point earners |
| | 1 ROM | | 118 ROM |
| | 1 winner | | 27 AQHA Champions |
| | Earnings of $1,098 | | 2 World Champions |

### Maternal Grandsire AQHA Summary:

1,618 foals from 211 mares
309 performers:

| | | | |
|---|---|---|---|
| Race: | 7 starters | Show: | 251 Point earners |
| | 4 ROM | | 72 ROM |
| | 4 winners | | 3 World Champions |
| | Earnings of $14,238 | | |

# *The Prologue*

As Charlie Ward, the cowboy who had cared for Doc Bar for over 20 years, stood beside his old pal in the alleyway of the San Francisco Cow Palace patiently awaiting an announcement for them to enter the arena, he studied Doc Bar. It amazed him how he could live with a person or an animal almost every day of his life and never notice the years robbing him of a youthful body or the tiredness settling in his eyes.

Standing there, with nothing to do but wait his time, no ranch chores dictating his every moment, no pressures flooding his mind, Charlie, for the first time in years, took a hard look at the horse standing nonchalantly next to him. Doc Bar stood relaxed, head hanging, mouth partially opened. The old man was beginning to show his age.

Horses photo
Doc Bar being honored at the Cow Palace at the age of 25. Shown holding the great stallion is Charlie Ward. Next are Mr. and Mrs. Stephen Jensen and Keith Christie, the artist who created the beautiful bronze sculpture.

*Shaking his head at the startling realization, Charlie hoped that the crowd waiting for them inside the coliseum would not be too disappointed with the stallion. Since he lived every day with Doc Bar, Charlie hadn't realized Doc Bar was not physically the same stallion he kept in his mind. The Doc Bar living there had a youthful appearance with firm muscles and bright, mischievous eyes. Those people in the bleachers who had not seen him for years might also have the image of a young Doc Bar in their minds. Hopefully, tonight they wouldn't be too disappointed. Maybe he shouldn't have brought Doc Bar, but come to think about it, those people crowded around his stall today had liked him.*

*Before another thought could enter Charlie's mind, the announcer began the stallion's introduction.*

*"And here ladies and gentlemen is the great stallion Doc Bar!"*

*There it was, Charlie's cue to walk the stallion into the arena. Taking a deep breath, he stepped the unassuming stallion inside.*

*As the lights dimmed in the coliseum, a spotlight searched the arena floor, finding Doc Bar and flooding him in a circle of light.*

*All of a sudden, it was as if Doc Bar, the 25-year-old stallion, remembered his glory days years ago in the Cow Palace and came to life. A stallion with his nostrils flared and the "prancy" walk of a young horse replaced the stallion which only moments before stood in the alleyway by Charlie. With his head held high, Doc Bar proudly paraded around the arena as the crowd, jumping wildly to their feet, thunderously applauded, giving the famous stallion a much-deserved standing ovation.*

*Charlie grinned as he began a trot of his own to stay beside the stallion. How could he have doubted the old guy? The stallion knew it; the crowd knew it too. Doc Bar was still the "King."*

# THE FINLEY YEARS

# 1

## *Blue-Blood Pedigrees For The Perfect Birth*

*It was just another work day for young Don Hemstrom, a cowboy on the Finley Ranch. Usually, he and Chewie (Jessie) Valdez broke and rode colts, but during breeding season his chores often changed from cowboying to truck-driving as he hauled mares to be bred at the ranches of stallions.*

*Today was one of those days.*

*After finding a halter, Don shuffled slowly in the brisk morning air to the mare trap. Although only in his early twenties, knee injuries and a broken leg from earlier years had forced him out of the cold climate of South Dakota to the hot dry air of Arizona. Still, brisk mornings like these worked on those knees, making movement sore and stiff for awhile. Scanning the mares as he neared the mare trap, Don immediately spotted Dandy Doll.*

*"Hope she don't want to play 'catch me if you can'," muttered Don, pausing to bend over to rub his knee. "This just ain't the morning."*

*It took only minutes, however, to find and load the mare and hours later Hemstrom pulled into the Lightning A Ranch on the north side of Tucson, Arizona, appropriately located next to the race track. The old Santa Fe-styled ranch, nestled peacefully amid mesquite trees and cactus and laying along a sandy wash, was home to the great racing stallion, Lightning Bar, the sire of Dandy Doll's future colt. The stallion, commanding a $500.00 stud fee, reigned from his own personal rock-hewn barn. The year was 1955.*

*Several months later Hemstrom once again made the journey to Tucson, this time to pick up Dandy Doll. The Finleys had chosen to leave her there until she missed a cycle, the only way to assure she was bred. The next year she gave birth to a tiny colt. The Finleys named him Doc Bar.*

\*\*\*

Nothing marked that day of birth as an eventful one. The only expectations were racing ones, evident by the pedigree of the parents; there were no dreams of revolutionized halter classes or dominating performance genes.

Yet, both the halter industry and the performance industry were destined for revival because of that day. Doc Bar, at that time, though, was just another colt born on the Finley Ranch for Don Hemstrom and Chewie Valdez to break.

"I don't remember Doc Bar being born," reminisced Tom Finley, the son of Jim Finley, owner of Dandy Doll. "We raised hundreds of colts, but he must have been born in one of the little traps around the corral. That's where we left mares to foal. Back then we never foaled any mare in a stall."

Although Finley does not remember the golden birth, he does remember the history surrounding the Doc Bar name.

"My dad's stepfather was Doc Gooden. Doc Gooden raised my dad, Jim Finley, from the time he was a little kid and Dad thought the world of his step-father.

"Doc Gooden was a horseman who was knowledgeable about sick animals and that's why they called him Doc. There weren't any vets back then, so he did the veterinarian work on the ranch. Instead of cattle, the family ran about 500 head of mares, raising horses for the army. Since they didn't sell them to the army until they were about three-year-olds, there was always something that needed doctoring. When Doc Bar was born, my dad thought about his step-dad and decided to name the horse 'Doc' after him. Of course, the 'Bar' part of the name came from his sire, Lightning Bar."

## The Finley Ranch Philosophy:

James Finley, along with his sons Tom and Jack, raised all-around horses, horses capable of entering a halter class and athletic enough to run down a race track. Their desire to achieve at more than one special activity with a horse, a novelty idea especially among race horses, sparked interest in the horse industry.

"Finley Ranches is a unique Quarter Horse breeding establishment for the Finleys produce horses that can do it all, " stated the April 1956 Arizona Stockman, "They show their horses, run 'em, cowboy on 'em and take 'em to the rodeos."

The do-it-all horses were, in fact, doing it all. At the Sonoita Quarter Horse Show in May, 1955, Finley Ranches took home eight ribbons and their mare, Annie Echols, was named Grand Champion mare of the show. Just the month before in Denver, Casbar, their 2-year-old stallion set a world's record of speeding 330 yards in 17.3 at the Rocky Mountain Quarter Horses Association Futurity.

In an article, "The Doc Bar Heritage" published in the June, 1979 Quarter Horse Journal, Tom Finley explained why the ranch strived toward a multiple-goal theory with their breeding program.

"We have always felt that a Quarter Horse should be an all-around athlete - the "Decathlon Champion" of horses - a horse bred to do everything. He must be an athlete with speed, muscle and the agility to perform in every type of event. We've never sacrificed conformation for speed; we possibly have at times sacrificed a little speed for conformation, but never the other way around." (p.83).

The breeding program philosophy was meant for all the colts born on the ranch, including Doc Bar. His story, and hence his ability, however, began years earlier with the purchase of Texas Dandy, a stallion sired by My Texas Dandy which had also sired some of the best known Quarter Horses of that time.

## The Maternal Grandsire, Texas Dandy:

The Finleys liked the style of several horses in Gilbert, Arizona - Clabber, Colonel Clyde, Lucky and Blue Bonnett - who were all sired by My Texas Dandy. Deciding that another My Texas Dandy stallion named Texas Dandy, which consigned to a Texas sale, most likely possessed similar qualities to these horses, the Finley boys wanted him for their breeding program. Therefore, after finishing a day's work, the two brothers knocked the dirt off their jeans, jumped into the truck and

Photo courtesy Quarter Horse Journal

Texas Dandy, the maternal grandsire of Doc Bar, was a beautiful Quarter Horse, standing 15 hands and weighing 1,200 pounds.

traveled all night to attend the Wharton Quarter Horse Sale where Texas Dandy was to be sold.

Even though they were bleary-eyed from the all-night drive, they still liked what they saw. When the gavel fell on the sale of four-year-old Texas Dandy, the Finleys had paid a record sale price of $5,250 to purchase the eye-catching, red-sorrel stallion.

"Texas Dandy had everything one would want to see in a Quarter Horse. He stood just 15 hands and weighed 1200 pounds. He had almost a classic head, a full blaze, little fox ears, and like so many My Texas Dandys, a sock on his hind leg. He was beautifully muscled but had style and refinement to spare."(Bob Denhardt:" The story Behind Doc Bar", The Western Horseman, July, 1986; p.13.).

As the backbone of much of the Finley breeding program, Texas Dandy produced colts for the short track, the show ring, the rodeo arenas and the multiple workings of a ranch, exactly what the Finley philosophy decreed. Little Egypt, a mare sired by Texas Dandy seven years before Doc Bar was born, proved to be an outstanding example of a dual-purpose horse. Running AAA her first time out as a two-year-old, Little Egypt set four world records for speed at the race track, and then went on to be AQHA's first and youngest AQHA champion. Another Texas Dandy offspring, Front Row out of Fleet F, first raced and then later won in calf-roping competition.

With trend setters like these emerging from the Texas Dandy genes, the Finleys decided to continue the pursuit of dual-purpose offspring using Texas Dandy mares and hedging their bet with a sire carrying additional race-horse genes. The choice was Lightning Bar.

### The Dam: Dandy Doll:

Dandy Doll, the Texas Dandy mare who was sent to Lightning Bar, had also won at the race track. Out of 21 starts, she had five firsts, two seconds and three thirds.

"Dandy Doll was a kind mare, no problems at all with her. She was a mare that won at the track at 220, 330 and 440, went all the distances," remembered Finley. "She was small which meant she had a lot of guts to run on out the quarter, and she was a nice-looking mare.

"Lightning Bar was doing well at the time, also. In fact, by then he had already produced quite a few runners, so the two of them seemed like a good match."

### The Racing Blue-Bloods:

Although Lightning Bar's racing career had been cut short by an injury, his pedigree read like racing blue-blood. His grandsire, Percentage, won 19 races and $42,187 in the days when nickels and dimes bought food and drink, while his grand dam, Myrtle Dee, held the track record for 5 1/2 furlongs at Coney Island Track in Cincinnati.

Lightning Bar's sire, Three Bars, after overcoming leg problems and a continual change of ownership, won his maiden start at Churchill Downs as a three-year-old, and continued to make a name for himself on the race track earning $20,840 before retiring to stud. Over the years his popularity inched his stud fee upward from $100.00 in 1945 to $10,000 in 1963.

"I've always said that you don't keep nothing but the good ones," said Melville Haskell, one of the founders of the American Quarter Racing Association, a former director of the AQHA and an ally for crossing Thoroughbreds with Quarter Horses. "And you don't use just any old Thoroughbred in your breeding program. There might be one stallion out of many a hundred that is fit to cross on a Quarter Horse. A good example of what you want is one like Three Bars...(he) had speed and conformation and...bred true, had the same type time after time." ("Three Bars," December 1979, p. 423, Quarter Horse Journal).

Photo courtesy Quarter Horse Journal

Doc Bar's sire, Lightning Bar, had his racing career cut short when he was injured. He is shown here, however, winning a 1953 race at Ruidoso Downs.

The Three Bars get affirmed the stallion's ability to pass along his talents. From his first crop, First Bar became a stakes winner, winning the George Drumheller Memorial Handicap at Longacres, Washington.

Another colt, Barred, started 15 times on recognized tracks. He won seven of those races, setting one track record, finished second in four of them and third in three. Glass Bars, a chestnut filly also from that first crop, only ran four races in her career, but she too, set a track record and incidentally, won all four times she ran. With each additional crop, the get continued racking up championships and honors.

Photo courtesy Quarter Horse Journal

Lightning Bar was the first offspring of Three Bars to succeed on and off the track. He was graded AAA on the track and was also named an AQHA Champion in the arena.

Lightning Bar, however, a son of Three Bars and the sire of Doc Bar, was the first of his offspring to succeed on and off the track. In 1953, Lightning Bar, graded AAA on the track, had 10 starts earning four firsts, three seconds and one third. Two years later, in 1955, he was named an AQHA Champion in the arena.

"Lightning Bar had the best hip and back leg that I have ever seen before or since," said Art Pollard. "... he was a sight to see! I think in halter he was only beaten one time." (Cutting, A Guide For the Non-Pro Competitor by Sally Harrison; Macmillan Publishing Co., p. 48.)

With such a pedigree, the union of Dandy Doll and Lightning Bar seemed to stack the deck for their offspring, Doc Bar, to possess exceptional speed highlighted by sizzling good looks and all-around ability. The records from other get by their ancestors showed great-grandsires passed their genes on to grandsires, who obligingly passed them on to sires. It stood to reason, then, that the genes would indeed transfer once again to another generation and Doc Bar would have it all. Planning, however, never comes with guarantees.

"We just didn't get what we had expected," sighed Tom Finley.

# 2

## *The Racing Years*

The Arizona sun drenched their shirts as Hemstrom and Valdez trotted young colts from the cotton fields, breaking them into a lope almost before the last plant was cleared. Day after day the two cowboys rode colts among the rows of cotton, watching the plants peep through the sandy loam, seeing the bolls blossom from tiny buds into white clouds of fluff. The acres of long straight rows made excellent training fields for young horses. When the sun's rays bounced from the sand, however, and boredom's tentacles reached for them from the monotony of uninterrupted paths, they always left the cotton fields behind for the refreshing groves of citrus fruit just down the road.

A mile and a half later the men slowed their horses to a walk, squinting from beneath well-worn hats at the orange fruit hiding among green foliage, expertly searching for just the right pick.

"These here look pretty ripe," commented Hemstrom, nodding toward a heavily-laden tree as he dismounted at the edge of the citrus grove. "Can't beat a tasty ripe orange on a hot day, can ya Chewie?"

Soon his pockets bulged with snacks and Don once again climbed into the saddle on Doc Bar. "Ya know," he smiled as he nudged the young stallion into a walk, "When I first started ridin' this horse, I was kind of embarrassed to get on him, what with him being so little and all. Bet he don't weigh an ounce over 750 pounds. But he's just been the nicest horse to break, gentle and quiet, no buck in him at all."

Then grinning as he watched his friend wrestle his broncy young stallion, he added, "bet you can't say that about yours!"

*One spring day in 1957, Charley Araujo, the renowned California horseman, made his annual trek to the Finley Ranch to look at the new-born foals. In the warm Arizona sun, the dapper Araujo, dressed in sharply creased pants and an open-necked shirt, looked every bit the master of horses as he leaned against the colt pens gazing at the young offspring.*

*"What's this colt?" questioned Araujo with a nod, his gaze resting on the smallest stallion in the bunch. To his critical, halter-trained eye the stallion's conformation was exceptional, a miniature replica of what he desired to lead into the ring.*

*Following Araujo's motion Tom Finley noted the colt under the horseman's studious stare. "That's Dandy Doll's colt - can't have a better Mama - and he's by Lightning Bar," he answered, joining Araujo at the pen. "Got some good racing blood from both sides so he should run. Good lookin' little thing, isn't he?"*

*"Yeah," acknowledged Araujo, shaking his head in agreement. Then turning slowly toward Finley, he added, "If you ever decide to pull him off the track, I'd sure like a shot at standing him."*

\*\*\*

Finley Ranches bred and bought hundreds of horses in their pursuit of race and halter champions as well as roping and ranch stock. Finley horses stood for both conformation and agility on the show circuits and Tom Finley credited that reputation to Texas Dandy.

"We never had raced a thick-neck, mutton-withered horse in all our 100 years of breeding," stated Finley, "but when we brought Texas Dandy back from South Texas and started showing his colts, they really made an impression on the judges."

It was a grandson of Texas Dandy, however, that impressed Charley Araujo. "Charley said Doc Bar was going to be one to stand when he was just a baby," mused Finley. "We bred them the way we believed; Charley then looked them over and told us which ones he thought were the best. He had a good eye for a horse, right from the time they were born."

On the Finley Ranch in the middle fifties, the colt pens which bordered two streets in Gilbert, overflowed with prospective champions. Doc Bar, although just another horse as a yearling, exhibited a curiosity about people and his surroundings which set him apart from the others. While other yearlings grazed or played, Doc Bar climbed the planks from which the pens were constructed and inquisitively sought the world beyond.

"Morning, evening, whenever, he'd put his front feet on those plank boards, stretch himself up and just stand there looking around," remembered Hemstrom. "He'd do that for a long time."

Although Doc Bar's antics sometimes got him into trouble, they also demonstrated his intelligence. "He was a smart horse," continued Hemstrom. " We had a chain with a snap on it that went around the gate and a fence post to lock it. One day, he climbed up there and got his foot hung in that chain, but he didn't pull back or fight it. He just stood there patiently and waited for someone to come get him out."

Even though the Finleys wanted horses that looked good, they still expected them to perform and Doc Bar seemed to fit well into that program. He possessed excellent conformation while his dam and sire lineage suggested he would definitely be a winner at the race track.

"I remember seeing him broke as a late yearling," stated Finley. "Like most of the young horses, everything seemed okay. It just looked like it would work, but then we really got a surprise when we tried to run him in January and February of his two-year-old year in Tucson," said Tom.

New Year's Day started the racing year off in Tucson. Finley had sought John Hazelwood, a quiet, nonchalant gentle man known for his talent in training race horses, to mold the racing talents of Doc Bar. When it came time to debut the young stallion, a young jockey named E. King donned the Finley colors and rode Doc Bar in several races including the Futurity at Rillito Park.

Even with Hazelwood's expertise and King's aptness, however, with each race, the hopes of racing championships for Doc Bar faded more and more. It was an age when many races were timed by stop watches and even those that used electric timers were only accurate to a tenth of a second.

Nevertheless, with four attempts at the track, Doc Bar, rated only as an A runner, had won a meager $95.00. In fact, according to Bruce Beckman in "Doc Bar: Life at the Top of the Hill" in the Quarter Horse Journal, "in his last race out, in 1958, he ran next-to-last in a 330-yard futurity trial, beaten by 8 1/2 lengths." (Dec. 90, p. 36)

Disillusioned, Tom Finley ended the racing career of Doc Bar. The Finley creed, however, deemed that they pursue another avenue with the stallion. Tom Finley, however, disapointed with their racing prospect though, preferred to cash in their chips.

"I decided I was going to get rid of him and I tried once to sell him to Lee Berwick."

Berwick, now an owner of the Delta Downs Race Track in Vinton, Louisiana, and a past President of the American Quarter Horse Association, remembered that proposal. "Tom offered me the horse for $30,000 and back then that was all the money in the world!" remembered Berwick.

Indeed, it was. That year, 1958, 87 cents bought a pound of coffee, $59.50 purchased four tires, $188.00 brought home a Frigidaire refrigerator and $30,000 bought a nice home.

"I had a bunch of daughters of Red Miller and I needed a horse to breed them to," continued Berwick. "Although I'd just sold a half brother to Doc Bar for $22,500, that was also all I could pay for another horse; so, I had to let the offer go.

"I was real keen on him though, and kept a picture of Doc Bar in my desk drawer at my office. I thought about that horse a lot. He was kind of a round-bodied horse, a real nicely balanced horse with eye appeal. I wanted him pretty bad."

Unable to sell the stallion, the Finleys decided to once again show him, but this time in halter. "We showed a lot of our colts while they were running," remembered Tom. "Little Egypt won Grand Champion one night and the next day she set a record on the race track, so showing our race horses wasn't anything unusual."

Approximately a year later in the summer of 1959, while Finley had Doc Bar at a Tucson show, opportunity began softly knocking for the young stallion.

"Charley (Araujo) and I went to the Tucson Quarter Horse Show and Tom was there with Doc Bar," remembered Marten Clark, a friend of both Finley and Araujo. I thought he was a nice horse. He had a nice hip and lot of stifle and tight tendons. We were concerned about his size, though, if he was big enough, but Charley wanted to try the horse."

When the show ended, Araujo and Clark, who had extra room in their trailer, loaded Doc Bar and Charley took the stallion to his Coalinga, California, ranch. Finally, Araujo had gotten the horse that had interested him as a weanling several years earlier. For Tom Finley it would be the last time that he would ever see the stallion.

Later, after parting with Clark, the hot dusty ride on to Coalinga gave Araujo plenty of thinking time. There was just something about this Doc Bar horse. He felt it deep inside, but couldn't put into words what he felt. In fact, bringing a horse with racing blood to his ranch went against everything he had ever preached. Still, this one was different. He had picked good horses before, and he knew with this one that he'd done it again.

That trip to Coalinga marked a turning point in Doc Bar's life. In the hands of Charley Araujo, the stallion would bury the stigma of a racing failure and replace it with accolades for revolutionizing the halter industry. At that time, however, for Araujo and Doc Bar, success was an unseen future. It was just another day.

Photo by Western Livestock Journal

Doc Bar's racing career was short lived as he only ran a grade A, winning a meager $95. In his last race out, in 1958, he ran next-to-last in a 330-yard futurity trial, beaten by 8 1/2 lengths.

# THE ARAUJO REGIME

# 3

## *Charley Araujo*

*Only a hint of dawn filtered through the kitchen window as Charley Araujo sat at the table, legs crossed, sipping another cup of coffee. Staring at the slowly changing sky, he waited patiently for the subsiding of a winter storm. The window pane rattled defiantly at the howling wind, its clatter breaking an otherwise stark silence that enshrouded the room. Charley Araujo waited, enjoying his coffee, cursing the wintry cold.*

*Just down the road, the branches of Tamarack trees scattered sparsely around his barn bent low, almost sweeping the hodge-podge of railroad ties haphazardly forming horse pens. Above them, loose tin popped noisily in resistance to the weather. Araujo shifted uneasily in his chair as he thought about the horses at his barn.*

*Still, he waited as the ticking seconds slowly unveiled the day. Storms did not fit Araujo's schedule, although his quiet demeanor masked his underlying agitation. Outside lay hours of breeding duties. Several of his Poco Tivio mares needed breeding to Doc Bar and that was just the first chore. In addition, owners had swelled the number of mares on his ranch, wanting them bred to Poco Tivio, Jimmie Reed and other stallions he was standing. Breeding just didn't allow time for rainstorms.*

****

Charley Araujo knew horses. His olive complexion, receding chin and dark eyes portrayed him as just another ordinary man, yet underneath that pretense lay extraordinary talent. Araujo possessed a photographic memory and a gift for recognizing and training good horses. Quiet in some ways, a gregarious conversationalist in others, when the subject turned to horses, Araujo commanded the title of premier horseman of California.

**Charley Araujo in 1961**

As a horse-trader he manipulated his talents, rising like cream to the top in showing, judging, buying, and breeding horses. In fact, few horse-traders could do as well as he with the challenge of finding hidden prospects and then molding them into blue-ribbon winners. It was something at which Charley was a master and the master believed he could mold Doc Bar, then an anonymity, into another one of his blue-ribbon winners.

## Early Years

Charley Araujo, born in Paso Robles, California, on November 11, 1908, one of four boys in a family of twelve children, lost the frivolity of youth at an early age, forced instead to learn about work and horses. During the era of his childhood, large families were an advantage since the more children, the more working hands. The Araujo family, like others, needed all of those hands to help make the money to buy flour and beans. Araujo reminisced about his youth with Anna Robertson in her article "Charley Araujo, Lifetime Student of Good Horseflesh" for the Quarter Horse Journal.

"I guess I must have been about 9 when I first ran the horse power on the hay baler. That was one of the things kids could do the youngest and it wasn't hard work - just tiresome for a little kid trying to keep the horses moving round and all day in the hot sun. How I used to wish for the baler to break down!

"I know that before I was 12, I was handling a team and loading and hauling grain. I hauled grain into San Miguel, a three day trip from the ranch" (July, 1972, p. 54).

Araujo dropped out of school at an early age, not uncommon for boys in the early 1900's. He then roped and rodeoed, and when the money ran out, cowboyed on ranches such as the San Simeon Ranch owned by millionaire publisher William Randolph Hearst and the McVitty Syndicate Ranch in the Cholame Hills. Those ranches became classrooms for young Charley who was receiving a cowboy education with cowboys as teachers.

"I learned more about horses from Ted Gilbert than any one man in my life," he stated in Robertson's article, referring to the superintendent of the McVitty Syndicate Ranch. "He knew about horses and he knew how to train them. Lots of guys are around horses all their lives and never really know about them - what makes them tick." (Charley Araujo: Lifetime Student of

Good Horseflesh, p. 54).

Under Gilbert's continual prodding, Charley polished a gifted talent with horses and soon he emerged more an equine artisan than just a working horseman. Like all good artists who develop an eye for their work, he saw in the weanlings' future, muscled-maturity, while others only saw leggy colts.

While ranch work just meant a paycheck to other cowboys, for Araujo, the long hours offered opportunities to refine his uncanny sixth sense about horses. Later, that sixth sense propelled him into selecting and showing the best horses in California while simultaneously aiding him in sculpting an intense breeding program to produce his own fine offspring. In essence, it made him the premier horseman of California.

## Building A Reputation

When the 1930's rolled around, Araujo left cowboying and other periodic oil-field jobs behind and determinedly struggled instead to build a horse business of his own. To do so, he tackled any equine-related work that would make a dollar. He stood the stallion Little Ben C, a grandson of Ben Hur, broke rank 4- and 5-year-old horses for $15.00 a week and later formed a partnership with horseman Lyle Christie, owner of Cantua Creek Ranch.

Araujo's role in the partnership was to buy horses with which he could win in the halter arena. He liked Joe Reed breeding, and, therefore, one of his first purchases was Catechu, a stallion by Joe Reed. The purchase was a successful one since in 1944, when California held its first Quarter Horse Show in King City, Catechu, with Araujo at the shank, won Grand Champion stallion. The championship established a trend he continued to weave with good horses for years to come.

Many owners and trainers coveted Araujo's ingenuity and talent while others praised it. His friend, Marten Clark, a past American Quarter Horse Association president, was one of those who attributed his own success in the Quarter Horse industry to Araujo.

"I think Charley was an outstanding breeder of horses. He possessed the ability to look at a foal, even if it was only a day old, and analyze what that foal would be like down the road. He also had a lot of talent breaking horses with the old style, intuitively knowing what made a horse good and what made him last. And he was hell on pedigrees! He just had a knack for knowing which bloodlines should be crossed to develop a particular kind of horse."

Besides breeding and training horses, Araujo added judging to his list of professions, wielding the pencil over open shows when judges' cards were only a glimmer in the future. His credentials continued to spread among horse shows, becoming so respected that in 1949, the American Quarter Horse Association appointed him inspector for the northern California/northern Nevada district. That year he also became an AQHA judge.

Since the two professions often kept Araujo away from his own bed at night, numerous times he stopped over at the home of his good friends, Floyd and Beverly Boss of Fresno, California, and slept on their couch. Beverly Boss considered those visits golden opportunities to gleen bits of knowledge from a master.

"Any time he came to stay with us and we had a new colt, I'd ask him to look at it. It didn't take long before I learned to watch what he'd do. He'd walk around and around the colt, looking him over and the expression on his face told you what he thought. If he smiled, it was a good one. Otherwise he wouldn't say anything, just shake his head."

A non-committal answer to a horse incapable of meeting Araujo's lofty standards typified his character. Intelligent and thoughtful with a subtle wit, he rarely criticized others or their animals, yet stood firmly in his own beliefs about horseflesh. Neither did he care, though, for others to argue with him about his opinions.

"If you carried on too much of a discussion with Charley, he'd call it arguing, and he hated that!" laughed Dave Jones, now a Floridian saddle-maker who once was hired by Araujo's partner, Lyle Christie, to help Araujo. "He liked sharing what he thought with people, but he didn't like you to hassle him. You had to know how to talk to Charley."

To Floyd Boss, a farrier, Araujo's behavior was just that he respected the professions of others and expected the same respect for his. "I went over to shoe Doc Bar after Araujo first got him," said Floyd, giving an example. "He went and got the horse from his stall and brought him over to where I was shoeing. So, I stood up and looked the horse over, then asked Charley how he wanted him shod. He just looked at me and said, 'you shoe him, I'll show him.' I liked that about Charley."

The friendship between trainer and farrier deepened over the years and often they spent hours talking horses. "I remember asking him one time, 'what makes you remember animals so well?'" continued Doss, "and he said, 'when we were little kids, strangers would come by and water their horses. We didn't have anything else to do but to look at 'em so I just got to studying them.'"

Aruajo's memory impressed everyone who came in contact with him. "I judged with him lots of times," remembered Jack Brainard of Gainesville, Texas. "He had the most unbelievable memory I've ever seen. I don't think there's ever been a judge as good as Charley Araujo; he knew what he liked and how to find it.

"In those days," continued Brainard, "we would sometimes judge 60-80 horses in a pleasure class and when we got through, everybody came and asked about their horse. Now it's hard to remember 60 different horses, but he could, and he'd talk to everyone of those people about their horses."

Araujo's authoritative explanations with contestants, plus his gift of memory, made him a popular judge. Before long, in addition to the AQHA judging card, he carried the American Horse Show Association card and the National Cutting Horse Association card, judging not only in the United States but in Canada and Guatemala as well.

When Araujo, the great horseman, finally connected with Doc Bar, the racing failure, an equine revolutionary ball began softly rolling. Before gaining momentum, however, it encountered several rocky roads.

## Problems With Doc Bar

After Doc Bar moved to California, he remained for three years under the hand of Araujo. The trainer, a noted winner of numerous stock horse reining classes, had visions of showing Doc Bar as a reiner.

"Charley wanted to show him in some of the big reining associations where there was a lot of money," remembered Beverly Floyd. "The horse had a great stop and he could slide a mile and even spin either way 'round and 'round, but he just couldn't change leads behind; no way in the world. Charley would lope him into a ditch where he had to come out angle ways; still, he wouldn't change leads. He worked and worked with that horse because everything else about him was as perfect as it could be, except for changing leads."

Searching for the answer, Charley put Jack Brainard on Doc Bar's back. Not only did Brainard and Araujo often share judging duties, Araujo's steely, dark eyes frequently marked Brainard's runs when he sat in the saddle. Hence, knowing his friend's talents, he asked Brainard to ride Doc Bar.

"We'd been off judging and I stayed with Charley a lot when we did that," reminisced Brainard. " When we got in that night, Charley said to me, 'You know, I've got a really nice horse at the barn but he's bad to get to change leads. I want you to try him.'

"The next morning Charley put Doc Bar in a snaffle bit and I rode him. He wasn't studdy or squealy; in fact, he was a nice-mannered, cute, little horse. He had a pretty neck, pretty head and stood square on his feet. When I rode him, though, I found he was short-strided and extremely dead in his sides. I'd stick him with a spur and he wouldn't even grunt; he wasn't sensitive in the mouth either.

"I was ridin' him out on the open flat where it was dry and dusty - Charley didn't have a pen to ride him in - and I finally got him loping, pulled his head around, squared him up, then stuck him with a spur and sent him the other direction. He just kind of wobbled into a canter, though. I tried it again and he did the same thing again.

"You can always make a horse change leads if you run him fast enough and lengthen his stride," continued Brainard. "So I sent him around there fast and he had to really work at that! Finally, when I picked up on him to change leads, I really had to pick him up high to get him to do it. I got maybe four out of ten tries and that's not very good."

Just like his racing career, Doc Bar's reining career ended in failure. There was always the pressing need to pay the rent and keep the electricity on, so the amount of time Araujo had to work with the horse dictated his plan with Doc Bar as much as the horse's insipid acquiring of changing leads.

"So much of it was the time, the mentality of those years," acknowledged Araujo's friend, Marten Clark. "Charley rode Doc Bar some, but he never worked him on cows. Since

Doc Bar wasn't a natural at changing leads, Charley was disappointed in the athletic ability of the horse. I rode him once and Doc Bar was the kind of horse that wanted to do something. That was just never applied to the area of his interest."

## A New Strategy

Araujo, by now known for his intuitive horse wisdom in the equine industry and needing to make a living, refused to give up on the stallion. Instead, he returned to the arena with 3-year-old Doc Bar, but this time, instead of stock horse reining classes, he took him to the halter classes.

"I had never heard or seen Doc Bar until Charley started showing him at halter," remembered trainer Don Dodge. "He showed up with this cute little horse and started beating everybody and that'll make you look! Until then, though, the horse was really an unknown quantity."

Out to erase that anonymity, Araujo meticulously chose the halter ring as the proving ground for Doc Bar's breeding program. Before long, the combination of a noted showman at the end of the lead rope with a horse whose conformation was unique to the halter class altered the guidelines for a halter horse champion.

Until Doc Bar, and later his get, stepped into the ring, it had been a different era for halter horses. They carried the genes of work horses, of raw-bone plow horses with little refinement or grace and horsemen accepted these animals that resembled the horses of their parents. The ancestors of the horses in the ring had worked the range or plowed the fields and then carried families to town for Sunday services. With the coming of Doc Bar, however, the look of the halter horse changed, closing a chapter in halter history and beginning a new one.

Change, though, nurtured complaints. Critics agreed Doc Bar, and later his get, were pretty, but questioned their ability to perform. Complaints never bothered Charley, whose answer flowed easily to Anna Robertson in her article "Charley Araujo" for the Quarter Horse Journal.

"I don't worry about that kind of talk. It takes time for a sire to get real 'doers' in the arena....I've found that whenever somebody is knocking my horses, there's usually a reason and the reason is that my horses are winning. And the thing you've got to remember is, if they're knocking my horses, they're thinking about them." (July 1972, p. 66.)

Between the years of 1960-1962, Araujo carried Doc Bar to shows all over California. Selectively, though, he chose shows with status, maximizing each show's prestige to gain the best visibility for his horse, mapping a plan to build the name of Doc Bar.

His strategy succeeded. Araujo, showed him in 15 shows. Doc Bar earned 12 first-place ribbons, three seconds, nine Grands and one Reserve and earned 36 halter points. ("Celebrated Doc Bar Passes On," <u>Southwestern Horseman</u>, Sept. 1992, Sec. A, Vol. 5, No.5).

All the while, at home, Doc Bar's breeding program was well under way. In the near future lay a grand slam win of both him and his offspring that would solidify the stallion's breeding career and hence retire him from the ring. The rocky road to stardom was getting smoother.

Photo by Ford's Photography

Charley Araujo winning at halter with Doc Bar. The pair altered the guidelines for a halter horse champion.

# 4

## Perceiving the Gold

*The stagnant air, heavy with the smells of horse manure, coliseum-sweat, and aging boards, created a sharp contrast to the fresh, clean-cut showman and his immaculately groomed horse standing at attention in the middle of the coliseum floor. As heat rising from the sandy arena mixed with the acrid air, it created a sweltering combination for the class of exhibitors, causing sweat to seep onto the shirts of other exhibitors and horses.*

*Yet, Charley Araujo and Doc Bar, as still as statues in the line-up, radiated a cool confidence that belied the caustic conditions of the day. This was show time, and Charley Araujo had come to win. It wasn't a time to think of weather or slow judges or other competitors. It was a time to think of winning and acting like a winner, something even Doc Bar seemed to understand.*

\*\*\*

While Araujo knew horses, he also knew business, and although horses spoke to his heart, profits spoke to his head. By the time he brought Doc Bar to his ranch, his breeding business already helped place meals on his table. No longer did he have to search the country for horses to break to help pay the rent. With the breeding business prospering, it just made sense to him to add another stallion to those he already stood.

For years, Araujo adamantly preferred Quarter Horses with their muscled power over Thoroughbreds, but when his equine-intuition saw dollar signs in Doc Bar, passionate blood preferences took a back seat to the persuasion of profits.

Dave Jones remembers with great amusement when Araujo got Doc Bar. "Even after I quit working for Charley, I stayed in touch with him. He didn't like running horses, so when I'd talk to him on the phone or wrote to him about different horses, he'd grumble, 'That one's got too much running horse in him for me.'

"Later on, he was judging in Pennsylvania where I was, so I went by to speak to him," continued Jones. "The first thing he said to me was, 'Hey, I just leased the prettiest horse I ever saw!' That's when he told me about Doc Bar. To hear him bragging on the horse was really funny to me because of Doc Bar's racin' blood and I wanted to tease him and say, 'That's too much running horse!', but I knew better!"

As soon as Araujo brought the stallion to Coalinga, he began breeding him. Although Araujo had his own mares to breed, he needed outside mares to help build a name for Doc Bar as well as to feed Araujo's bank account. Therefore, while enacting a breeding program, he also enacted an advertising program using the show ring to do so.

Home for the breeding program, though, raised the eyebrows of many mare-owners. While the string of stallions standing at Araujo's operation oozed perfection, the ranch itself oozed neglect. That, however, didn't bother Araujo; in fact, he preferred his ranch that way.

Araujo leased his land from the Southern Pacific Railroad Company and, therefore, conveniently relied on left-over railroad ties to build corrals. Rusted tin often retrieved from the city dump bravely fought to defend horses from the blistering sun and pelting rains. Araujo, a dapper dresser himself and a man who groomed horses to perfection, theorized that if his ranch looked profitable, the railroad company would increase his rent. Such thinking justified his use of materials and his unkempt facility. Tight with a dollar, he took no chances.

Saving money did not apply, however, when it came to feeding his prized boarders.

"Charley was a full feeder of his show horses, plenty of hay and sweet feed for them. He had a series of little horse barns with runs on them," remembered Dave Jones. "Everyday you took this wagon around to the different barns, cleaned out the old hay - those alfalfa stems were fed to the working horses - and gave them some fresh hay. We had those huge three-wire bales and we fed plenty of it."

Those barns and corrals of railroad ties in Coalinga became home to Doc Bar in 1959 and regardless of the ranch conditions, he fared well.

"Until Charley started breeding Doc Bar, the Poco Bueno type-horse was winning at the halter shows," remembered Tom Finley. "All of a sudden, when the Doc Bar colts were weanlings, they started winning and before long they changed the pattern of the halter horse in California."

Doc Bar's personality made combining the roles of breeding and showing easy. The stallion, an easy breeder, also adapted agreeably to the show limelight. Still, it took a while, however, for breeders to adapt to Doc Bar and haul their mares to Coalinga.

"Nobody wanted to breed to him at first, " remembered trainer Bobby Ingersoll of Pleasant Grove, California. "Charley stood him for $300, but he still had a hard time getting people started on him. Charley, though, had a lot of faith in him. Thank goodness for that."

Nine owners, most of whom had Araujo connections, bred mares to Doc Bar and in 1960, the next year, eight fillies and one stallion were born. Araujo, himself, owned one of the mares, Mansita, sired by Jimmie Reed who also stood at the Araujo Ranch. She foaled Mansilla Bar, who would later do well in the spotlight.

From his partnership with Lyle Christie, he bred Red Jane C, a full sister to Poco Bueno, which produced a sorrel filly named Janie Bar, another name later to be reckoned with in show circles. Christie also bred his outstanding mare Lucky Bet by Lucky Blanton, which Araujo rode to numerous winners' circles, and named her filly Bet's Barita.

Puss Cat, owned by Cecil Johnson of Tempe, Arizona, and connected distantly to Araujo through the stallion Catechu that Araujo stood, foaled a sorrel filly, Doc's Sassy Cat. A similar story surrounded Clytivia who delivered the filly Tivia Bar. The mare, owned by Ed Burgson of Sonora, California, was sired by Poco Tivio, who was owned by Araujo. Two other mares bred to Doc Bar that first year were owned by Nancy E. Brooks of Napa, California. Trape Ann foaled Miss Doc Bar and Kingslee by King foaled Miss Doe Bar. The eighth filly, Bar Mist, was born to Cinnamon Deck by Quarter Deck, owned by Henry Edwards of San Jose, California.

The only stallion born from that first group, a palomino named Barlet, was out of Nevada Starlet by Nevada King and owned by Marten Clark of Soledad, California, a good friend of both Araujo and Tom Finley. Clark's faith in Araujo's equine perception led him to agree to breed his outstanding mare to an unproven stallion with no colts on the ground.

"I decided to breed to Doc Bar because we were trying to get away from the bull-dog type, muscular horse. Doc Bar had a pretty head and neck and he had style and refinement. We thought this would be a good change, more to what the model horse should look like. We weren't even thinking about the working end of the breeding that came a long later," said Clark.

When Marten's young stallion, Barlet, was born, however, his conformation was so strikingly different from the show-ring of that day, Clark had concerns about Barlet's future.

Photo by Potts

Lucky Bet, a daughter of Lucky Blanton, which Araujo took to numerous winners' circles. Owned by Lyle Christie and Araujo, she was bred to Doc Bar, with the resulting filly being Bet's Barita.

"I said to Charley, 'Charley, I'm not too happy with this colt. He doesn't look like he's got enough muscle to me.' But Charley very confidently told me to just wait and let time take care of it, pointing out we were getting more stretch, more refinement and that was what we were looking for."

Barlet certainly did not disappoint his owner, who later make quite a name for himself in the halter circles. First, however, he made it in the movies.

"When he was two-weeks old, they used him in shooting a Disney movie, called "The Horse With The Flying Tail," which was about a jumping horse called Nautical," remembered Marten. "It won the Academy Award for "Best Documentary Feature Length" that year."

The cross of Nevada Starlet and Doc Bar sparked magic and a year later Barlet, as well as three of the fillies from Doc Bar's first crop, Bar Mist, Janie Bar and Mansilla Bar, set the stage for Doc Bar get in the AQHA arena. In addition, under the guidance of Glynda Packer, Janie Bar later excelled in cutting as well, finishing eighth in the 1973 NCHA Non-Pro Top Ten.

Again in 1961, Doc Bar received only eight mares to his court, but all from a different group of owners than the 1960 breeders. Still considered unknown and unproven himself, his get having yet to debut in the arena as well, mare owners remained skeptical.

From that year's breeding, five fillies and three colts were born, of which three entered the show arena. Al Dolcini bred Teresa Tivio by Poco Tivio to Doc Bar and she foaled a bay filly named Fizzabar. Beany Bug, owned by Luna Mia Ranch of Canoga Park, California, produced Doc's Bug Bar, a chestnut stallion. Nelly Bly by Red Joe, owned by S. W. Talbot of Riverbank, California, produced another chestnut stallion named Tripolay Bar. Interestingly, one of Nelly Bly's daughters, Bar Maid F by Bartender II, had produced Dandy Doll, the dam of Doc Bar.

"Trip," as Tripolay Bar was affectionately called, excelled wherever he competed. Besides winning the Yearling Halter Futurity at the San Francisco Cow Palace in 1962, he earned his Register of Merit in racing the first time out. He also demonstrated his cutting expertise long before entering a training program, according to Lyn Jank in the article "Blood Will

Tell" for the <u>American Horseman.</u>

Trip "... did his own cutting Tripolay style, when he was stalled at the (race) track. Whenever mice came in to steal some feed, Trip would corner them every time. It was literally the Cat and Mouse game with a horse instead of a cat." (Dec 1981, p. 22)

Unfortunately, the stallion became cast in the stall less than 24 hours after he entered cutting training, an accident that caused two fractures and a large, triangular chip in his leg. With proper care, he healed though and later earned his AQHA Register Of Merit (ROM) and became an NCHA money earner.

In 1961, while mares who had been to the court of Doc Bar foaled the stallion's second group of offspring, the halter class players began taking a second look at Doc Bar when Marten Clark entered Barlet in the Pacific Coast Quarter Horse Association Futurity held in Fresno. Barlet swept the Futurity and then later earned the title of Supreme Champion, becoming statistical proof that, not only was Doc Bar revolutionizing the California halter classes, but he was passing the genes on to his offspring. Just as important, the judges were watching.

Dave Jones remembers the day that Araujo, with his uncanny "sixth sense" about horse flesh, taught him a lesson about using his head in the horse business rather than following his heart.

"Poco Tivio was Charley's love of life. Years after I quit working for him, I went back to buy two Tivio colts. I was there about five days getting a railroad car ready to ship the horses back to Pennsylvania, so we had plenty of time to talk. I remember the day I brought up that running horse stuff.

"There was a pen of Doc Bar colts and a pen of Poco Tivio colts almost side by side and Charley's ol' dog Joe was laying out there between 'em. I asked Charley why, after he'd been against race-horse blood for so long, that he stood a horse that had racin' blood in him. He said, 'Ya know, I'd have to sell five of the Tivios for what I can get for one Doc Bar. The primary thing about being in the horse business is that you have to have the popular horse.' "

The horseman, who knew a dollar when he saw it, also knew how to get it in his bank account.

# 5

## *Poco Tivio*

*Daily, Beverly Boss went to the barn to brush Poco Tivio. The stallion, left to her and her husband, Floyd, at the time of Charley Araujo's death, had become a precious treasure to her since coming to live with them. She cherished Poco Tivio as much as the couple cherished their note from Annie Araujo that accompanied his arrival. It read "Poco Tivio - my gift to you-at Charley's request. May he serve you well."*

*Beverly gave him grain while brushing him and he nudged her gently when he felt the grooming time should be over. A gentle horse, the lady never tied him; in fact, never even haltered him for his daily brushing, even though he still stood to mares. It was evident that Poco Tivio and Beverly Boss shared a mutual affection.*

*When he died, the Bosses buried Poco Tivio in their front yard, a white picket fence surrounding the grave and a St Francis Statue standing nearby. The front of his tombstone told the necessary information, but its back which read, "A true friend" told what was in their heart.*

\*\*\*

A life, whether it be human or animal, rarely stands alone. Like building blocks, it interacts with other lives, holding some up, leaning on others, influencing, being influenced and fusing together.

Such is the story of Poco Tivio, a building block in Doc Bar history. Many mares sired by this great stallion wove themselves into Doc Bar's life, creating a registry of winning get that bolstered Doc Bar's climb to fame. Poco Tivio's own legacy sheds light on the rich heritage in the Doc Bar/Poco Tivio-mare cross. California trainer Don Dodge, once an

Charley Araujo and Poco Tivio

owner of Poco Tivio, played several roles in the lives of the two stallions.

"I bought Poco Tivio in 1951 for $10,000 when I only had $12,000 in my pocket," remembered trainer Don Dodge with a chuckle. "I was not a stud horse man, but I decided I could make $300 a breeding from him, so I tried it. It was the pits for me, though. I didn't know anything about it and he was a shy breeder, anyway. A bird would fly over and he wouldn't breed, so I wanted out of the breeding business!

"Now, when I don't want to own a horse, you can buy him; in fact, you better not open your mouth or you're gonna own him!" he laughed. "I'm a firm believer that the first loss is the best loss, so I tried to sell him for $4,500, but I couldn't get anybody to buy him. When that didn't work, I decided to bridle Poco Tivio and show him in bridle classes - events like our reined cowhorse classes today - and get him some more exposure. Sure enough, he did well."

About the time that Charley Araujo, judging a Texas show, was impressed by the great stallion Poco Bueno, his friend, Don Dodge in California, decided to sell Poco Tivio. Since Poco Tivio was a son of Poco Bueno, Araujo was interested. The fact that Poco Tivio succeeded in the reined cowhorse classes sparked Araujo's curiosity all that much more.

"Charley Araujo was cowboying for a wealthy lady named Mrs. Lewis - she called him George," grinned Dodge, ruefully. "I had helped Charley get started judging, so we knew each other well. I wanted to sell this horse and he wanted to get into breeding, so Mrs. Lewis put up the money and I sold him to Charley for $7,500. I was tickled!"

As his grin widened, Dodge admitted, however, that the last laugh may have been on him.

"Of course, due to Charley's 'b.s.' and promotion and all the people he knew, he got some breedings to the horse and before long, they're both famous! Pretty soon he's judging all kinds of shows all over the country and without needing my help to get the job!"

## The Dam, Sheilwin:

A specific breeding program on the Waggoner Ranch, designed to breed Poco Bueno to mares from the Pretty Boy and

Blackburn cross, delivered Poco Tivio. As Phil Ray explained in his article "Poco Tivio" for the <u>Quarter Horse Journal</u>, "Poco Tivio's mother Sheilwin, represented the best of Waggoner Ranch breeding at that time. Her sire was Pretty Boy by Dodger by Harmon Baker. She was out of a mare by Blackburn, who was destined to become a leading maternal grandsire of AQHA Champions." (Feb. 1980, p. 171)

This cross usually bore mares with Blackburn sense and Pretty Boy looks. Pretty Boy, known to be a little broncy, marked his offspring with his superb conformation, overriding the rough, common appearance of Blackburn mares, while the Blackburn side of the cross delivered a level-headed temperament, erasing the rowdy behavior.

Poco Tivio

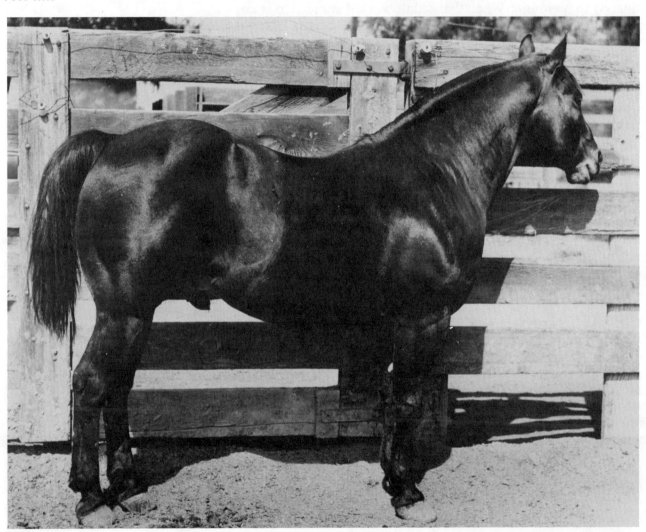

Five other great horses besides Poco Tivio came from this breeding program: Pretty Pokey, Poco Lena, Poco Champ, Poco Sandra and Poco Teddy. Although all of the Poco Bueno/Sheilwin progeny were excellent horses, their dam almost did not make the broodmare band. Sheilwin carried the right blood for the broodmare band, but she represented a backfire in the Pretty Boy/Blackburn breeding program, retaining, instead of losing, the Blackburn common appearance.

"I thought she was the plainest-headed, coarsest-made mare I had ever seen around the ranch," stated Pine Johnson in Bruce Beckman's "Legends" in the Quarter Horse Journal. Johnson trained horses for the Waggoner Ranch.

"If you looked at her, you wouldn't ever think of breeding her. Plus, she wasn't broke to ride; she was barely halter-broke! I told E. Paul (Tom Waggoner's son) that she wouldn't work for breeding. I would have never bred her myself."

As both Dodge and Johnson, later in that same article admitted, trainers can't always foresee the future of horses, even those they know the best. The coarse-haired, dun mare produced such outstanding foals that Waggoner built her a special barn and paddock.

Charley Araujo and Puro Tivio, one of the great sons of Poco Tivio.

## The Sire, Poco Bueno:

Sheilwin's first son, Poco Tivio, as well as her five other foals, were all by Poco Bueno, a son of the famous King P-234. Poco Bueno, who was foaled in 1944 on Jess Hankins Ranch in Texas, also lacked luster in his appearance as a young colt, sporting a drab brown coat with no outstanding markings.

Still, he blossomed by his yearling year and won his class at the July 4 Stamford yearling show, thus catching the eye of several breeders. When he later sold in the Hankins Brothers' first production sale, E. Paul Waggoner of Vernon, Texas, topped the sale with his $5,700 bid for the stallion. Poco Bueno went home to Sheilwin and in 1947, Poco Tivio was born.

Poco Bueno, which stood to many halter grand championships, also took to the sport of cutting under the guidance of Pine Johnson, as did his son Poco Tivio. Leslie Groves told of his cutting prowess and the growing interest in the stallion in "Legends: Poco Bueno" for the Quarter Horse Journal, stating, "Before long, Johnson was taking along Poco Bueno's first son, Poco Tivio. The crowd loved to see the sire-and-son team as one would cut and the other turn back, then swap positions" (April, 1994, p. 18).

When the Waggoners held their September, 1950 Production Sale, Poco Tivio, which was consigned to the sale, was purchased by Cliff Magers. The stallion's $5,000 purchasing price topped the sale. Magers continued the winning streak with Poco Tivio, both in halter and in cutting. Before another year was out, however, Don Dodge, then a California hunter and jumper trainer, purchased the stallion reportedly for the highest price paid for a cutting horse at that time. With the purchase of Poco Tivio, which he took home to California, Dodge moved the blood of King to the Pacific coast.

That same year, the American Quarter Horse Association started keeping show records. Poco Tivio, with Dodge in the saddle, continued to rack up points, now charted by the AQHA, and when the coveted list of horses winning the first AQHA Championships was released, the stallion headed the list.

It was a busy year for Poco Tivio. Besides competing in AQHA events, Dodge also carried him to NCHA competition where he finished the year sitting 6th in the NCHA Top Ten, having won $6,972.86.

Larry Thornton, from an interview with Dodge for an NCHA Cuttin' Hoss Chatter article titled, "Poco Tivio and the Broodmare Influence", wrote, "Dodge stated, 'Poco Tivio was different from the horse of today. He was heavier muscled and a good mover with lots of cow.' Dodge explained that in the early days of organized cutting, a rider needed a horse like Poco Tivio because of the ranker cattle... ranker because they were used as re-run cattle in the second go. Add to this situation that they used only one turnback man and you can readily see why Dodge was looking for a good-moving horse." (May, 1988, p. 80)

Again and again Don Dodge's horsemanship indelibly influenced the art of cutting. Besides introducing Poco Tivio's pedigree to the West Coast and riding him to numerous championships, Dodge, unknowingly at the time, helped modify the cutting horse industry during his short tenure as a breeder with Poco Tivio.

"When I bought Poco Tivio, I needed some mares to breed to him," said Dodge. "Leon Saylors, who lived about 30 miles from me, had two Blackburn mares and I made a deal with Leon to breed those two mares for the choice of the colts. When they were born, one was a stud colt and one a filly. By then, I was figuring out I didn't want any more studs, so I took the filly and named her Saylor's Little Sue. I bred her to Poco Tivio and named that filly Teresa Tivio after a lady I was seeing.

"Wouldn't you know it, that filly was a silly thing, scared of her own shadow! She'd do crazy things like crawl up the side of her stall and fall down! I didn't think she was any count so I stuck her in a sale and Arnold Dolcini, a dairyman, bought her for $800. Once again, I thought I'd done real good!

"She was barely broke to ride and she was pretty bad as a 2-year-old, so before long, Dolcini took her out of training. He bred her to Doc Bar and this silly filly I couldn't wait to get rid of the year before, started producing all these fantastic horses!"

Horses born from this union that excelled in the cutting arena included Fizzabar, an NCHA Hall of Fame horse and winner of $50,814.75; Nu Bar ($16,539), Boon Bar ($12,325), Doc's Remedy ($47,453), Doc Bar Gem ($8,683,) Doc's Haida ($67,305) and Cran Bar, NCHA Certificate of Ability, and Cal Bar ($10,426), NCHA Bronze Award, NCHA Top Ten.

## Growth Of the Tivio Influence:

Teresa Tivio and her get were just one of many Tivio mares bred to Doc Bar over the life of his stallion service. From the total offspring that Doc Bar sired, 72 foals were born to Tivio mares such as Teresa Tivio, Amiga Tivio, Bella Tivio, Candy Tivio, Clytivia, Dulce Tivio, Isla Tivio, Jameen Tivio, Jean Tivio, Lura Tivio, Miss Tibia, Poco Boots, Poco Quiz, Susie's Bay, Tasa Tivio, Tierra Tivio, Tonette Tivio and Tularosa Tivio.

The offspring of Poco Tivio sparkled with versatility. With a level-headed temperament, yet a flashy working style, they competed well in halter, pleasure, trail and cutting and then brought those traits to the Doc Bar union.

When Charley Araujo purchased Poco Tivio from Don Dodge in 1952, however, Doc Bar was not even born.

# THE JENSENS

# 6

## *The Jensens*

*Stephen Jensen strolled briskly out of his dental practice shortly after 12 noon, hurrying home for lunch. His mind already raced to the week-end ahead. It had been one of those hectic mornings in the office: an emergency, a couple of patients that took longer than he expected; just tense, tiring things that made him look forward all that much more to the week-ends, especially now that they owned the ranch.*

*Glancing at his watch, he mentally calculated the hours until he and Jasmine would be southbound for the Double J Ranch at Paicines, California. They rarely missed a weekend, even though the ranch was over a two-hour drive away and once you got there, you were almost an hour from milk and bread! In fact, they learned quickly not to forget the necessities of life when they went to Paicines.*

*A grin covered his face just thinking about owning a ranch. Who would ever have believed five years ago that now, in 1958, he not only owned one, but he couldn't wait for Friday afternoons to leave Orinda, California, behind and go to the Double J! Who would have believed five years ago that he, such an avid golfer, would be on the golf greens less these days so that he could be on a tractor more?*

*Yep. Life really was good.*

\*\*\*

It all started because of the "empty-nest syndrome." The silence in the home of Stephen and Jasmine Jensen in Orinda, California, echoed loudly from room to room after the Jensen children had all left home.

"I was at college back East," remembered Stephenie Ward, a daughter of the Jensens. "So was my brother, who had also gone back East to college. My sister, the youngest, was about to enter boarding school in Arizona and my other brother was in boarding school in Southern California. None of us were at home anymore so it was awfully quiet around the house for them."

Stephen, a 6-foot 2-inch, agreeable man, enjoyed making rounds on the golf greens, casting his rod from a fishing boat, or crouching in the woods, a hunting rifle resting against his shoulder. Jasmine Jensen, a tall, distinguished lady, possessed the same adventuresome spirit as her husband. As one child and then another left home, lessening parental responsibilities but bolstering the loneliness of a quiet household, the couple delved deeper into away-from-home activities.

## A New Hobby:

On one particular recreational trip south of Hollister, California, they fell in love with a quiet valley, cradled lovingly by mountains on each side and far from the confines of the city. Although the couple had never considered owning a ranch, the serenity of the Paicines area, plus dwindling home responsibilities in Orinda, enhanced the thought of owning a secluded retreat.

"They had actually come to this very ranch on a hunting trip, fell in love with it, and commented to their friends that if the ranch was ever for sale, they were interested buyers," explained Stephenie. "They had never owned a ranch and really knew little about either cattle or horses.

"Oh, he rode horses some on weekends as a member of the Sonoma County Trailer Blazers," she added, "but that was more to have fun with the boys rather than because he enjoyed riding. Mother had ridden some, too, since she showed hunters and jumpers when she was growing up, but they had never done anything serious with animals."

In only a short time the ranch became available and true to their word, the Jensens purchased the property, proudly dubbing it the Double J Ranch. For Stephen Jensen, a successful Orinda, California, dentist, weekends on the ranch in Paicines meant leaving behind his office with its persistent obligation to cleanliness and sterility.

After a week of hectic daily schedules and parades of patients, he plunged headlong into care-free week-ends complete with soft, worn clothes; timeless days and uncomplicated living. The ranch offered an almost diametrical lifestyle, the change was a sweet payment for long, stressful hours and city life.

"When they first bought the ranch, it was like a new toy and they loved being a part of it," smiled Stephenie. "Both of them enjoyed being out in the pasture, helping to bale the hay, doing the ranch chores. In fact, my dad just lived to get on a tractor. If all of the tractors weren't running when he came down, he got mad!"

## The Ranch Business:

Owning a ranch, even if it did provide escape from a routine of years and years of professional obligations, still meant work and responsibility. Taxes, land payments, insurance, and daily maintenance obligated the ranch to generate its own income and help guarantee future years of enjoyment. Shortly after settling into week-end ranch life, the adventurous Jensens quickly got serious about full-time ranch business.

For a while, the couple seriously considered going into the Hereford cattle business, but the Hereford cow finally lost out to the Quarter Horse. Neither profit nor profession solidified this final choice.

"The real reason they decided to go with horses rather than cattle," laughed Stephenie, "was because Mom thought baby colts would look better in the pastures around the house than baby cows!"

Jasmine's desire for esthetic charm cinched the choice of animals to subsidize the ranch income. Along with raising animals came the need to raise hay for feed, so while Stephen Jensen quickly jumped into the role of farmer, Jasmine Jensen ardently took on the role of equine student.

An eager pupil, she studied every piece of available information she could find on horses. She then visited with many "names" on the show circuits, learning about the horses themselves as well as the business of showing them. Pedigrees fascinated her and as her knowledge grew, she became more and more intrigued with their new business.

"My mother was probably more involved with the bloodlines of the horses than my father," continued Stephenie, "She made a study of them and became quite knowledgeable about pedigrees. Although Dad was interested in pedigrees and really enjoyed fooling with them, Mother was more serious about studying them! At that time in their lives, my parents were inquisitive novices in the horse business and both of them were thoroughly enjoying their new hobby."

While Dr. Jensen echoed his wife's enthusiasm about their horse business, his love for the ranch itself often precipitated horse-hunting excursions with her. Jasmine studied horse-sale books, highlighting the horses in them that interested her, marking the dates on her calendar to remind her to attend the sales. Undaunted that tractors, hay and fences deterred Stephen and being extremely independent, Jasmine, instead of canceling those trips, went alone.

"They'd make definite plans to go look at a horse and then something would come up at the ranch and Dad would feel that he just couldn't get away. It didn't bother Mother, though. She'd just take off by herself. She went to a lot of horse sales alone and bought horses," admitted Stephenie.

## Halter Fever:

At that time, the name of Charley Araujo, the halter-horse showman considered by many to be the most knowledgeable horseman on the West Coast, caught Jasmine's attention. Halter, raging supreme in the equine show circles, also piqued her interest and she soon purchased a mare that Araujo was showing. The mare, named Jameen Tivio, was the Jensen's first Poco Tivio filly.

Jameen Tivio, a 1956 bay mare, started her halter career in 1958, accumulating four points that year. The Jensens purchased her in February of 1959 after which she accumulated eight more points, some of them with either Stephen or Jasmine at the shank.

The mare, as with all of the Jensen animals, was more than just a show horse; she was a family pet, one that daughter Taga Jensen took back to college one year.

Photo by George Art

Stephen Jensen showing Doc's Loxie at the Cow Palace in 1962. The yearling filly was out of Ben's Loxie C by Ben C.

Several years later, in 1966, the mare returned to the show arena to add additional points to her total, accumulating 13 halter points in open competition. This all took place before she built an outstanding reputation as a broodmare.

"She was a nice halter horse, cute and little, and they really enjoyed showing her until halter horses started changing to the rangy, Thoroughbred look," remembered Stephenie. "She was their first show horse and eventually became a broodmare, even though they have purchased several other broodmares in between."

Overnight the Jensens emerged as prominent halter horse owners, notable both in appearance and ownership. Darryl Lund, an avid horseman who knew of the Jensens before leaving for the armed forces, remembered the confident aura the couple presented in the horse industry.

"They were very active in the Pacific Coast Quarter Horse Association when I went into the service. They were the distinguished people of the Quarter Horse world, always at the shows and always with good horses. After I got out of the service and came back to the Quarter Horse shows, they were still there, both poised individuals, showing horses with similar style. By then they had also bought Doc Bar and his offspring offered the same class and elegance you expected of the Jensens."

Stephen Jensen, finding guns to be a common interest with Doc Bar-breeder David Brown, developed an on-going friendship with the Minnesota horseman.

"The Jensens were very educated people," stated Brown as he spoke fondly of them. "Stephen was quite a nice man who had a certain mischievousness about him. We were both avid hunters, so he was naturally interested in guns and that bonded the two of us."

Photo by Ford's Photography

Knotty Bar, a 2-year-old son of Doc Bar out of Mansita by Jimmie Reed, winning at halter in 1967. Jasmine Jensen is shown with the trophy.

Life's circumstance molded much of the equine choices for the Jensens while the freedom to do what they wanted, rather than what they had to do, allowed those choices. When Jasmine Jensen purposely chose Charley Araujo to learn first-hand about horses, the developing friendship began a "domino effect" of equine circumstances.

Since Araujo was an avid halter-horse showman, he naturally influenced the Jensens' interest in halter horses. This, in turn, easily affiliated them with the halter industry. With expert guidance from Araujo, the Jensens were soon fixtures on the Quarter Horse Circuit, devoted to the industry and enthusiastic about the sport. With their purchase of Jameen Tivio from Araujo, they quickly became blue ribbon collectors and each thrill of winning spirited the desire to attend another show.

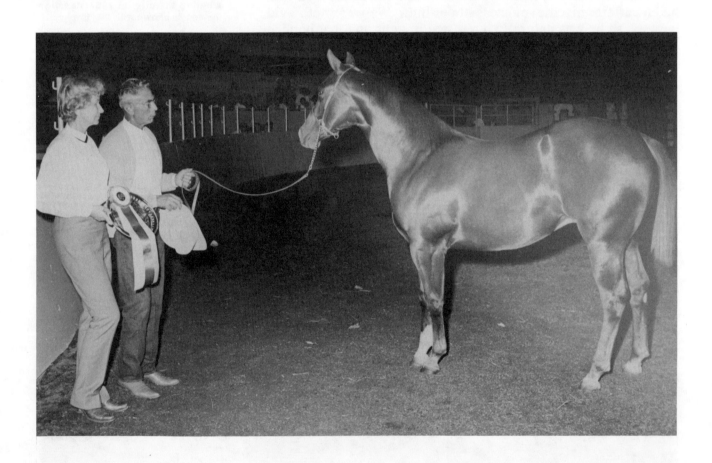

Jim Bar Araujo winning a halter class at the 1965 Cow Palace. The son of Doc Bar was Reserve Junior Champion Colt, first in the Yearling Colt class and was Superior Champion Futurity Colt. Shown at the shank is Charley Araujo. Jasmine Jensen is holding the awards. The 1964 stallion was out of Jimmette by Jimmie Reed.

Soon serious hunting and fishing trips gave way to hours at Quarter Horse events in which their growing number of horses competed. Their freedom to afford and show halter horses permitted the "domino effect" and Jasmine and Stephen Jensen settled comfortably into their role of show-horse owners.

But only for a while.

Just as freedom brings choices, it also allows for change. No one, at that time, however, envisioned another diametrical change in the Jensens lives, one that would take them from showing halter horses to breeding cutting horses. No one envisioned a change that would take them from owning a halter champ to owning the "Cutting King."

Ellinger Photo

**Jasmine Jensen with Docsen, a son of Doc Bar out of Miss Sen Sen.**

# 7

## *The Purchase of Doc Bar*

*As Jasmine Jensen scrubbed the potatoes she planned to cook for dinner, she once again mentally counted the number of guests who would be arriving shortly to spend the weekend. The ranch was a glorious place to entertain and now that she had completely redecorated the rambling old house and had enough bedrooms to accommodate a basketball team, she and Stephen frequently invited friends to Paicines to enjoy the tranquility of the country.*

*Those morning hikes on which she usually took the gals who visited, always brought them back tired, but somehow invigorated and refreshed. There was just something about walking here in the valley.*

*After completing pre-dinner chores, Jasmine hurried to the living room, where she fluffed the pillows and opened the blinds. Then, retrieving the dominoes and cards from a drawer, she carefully laid them out for the evening entertainment. All of their friends enjoyed bridge and dominoes and often laughter echoed well into the night from the ranch house when they had a hot game of cards going.*

*Now that the house was in order, it was time for a few ranch chores before their guests arrived. Slipping a sweater around her shoulders, Jasmine stepped out the back door and walked quickly toward the alfalfa field. Just this morning, she and Stephen had discussed the need to move the field's irrigation pipes and as the field came into view, she saw him and their daughter, Thea, already struggling to move them.*

*Pausing by a mare-pen to stroke a mare while she enjoyed the scene of father and daughter working together, she realized how fortunate they were to own this ranch. Now, if only they could get Doc Bar bought, it would be absolutely perfect!*

\*\*\*

Doc Bar easily captured the attention of Dr. and Mrs. Jensen as they traveled the Quarter Horse circuit. The stallion, an eye catcher with his graceful, refined conformation, stood out amid the rougher-type horses, especially with the Jensens' trainer-mentor Araujo showing him. Almost overnight, Doc Bar and then his get, infiltrated the winners' circles, abruptly revolutionizing the previous Poco Tivio-type, blue-ribbon thinking.

Interestingly, Charley Araujo, the owner of Poco Tivio, whose get had dominated the classes for so long, stood at the shank of Doc Bar and once again on the leading edge of the revolutionary change.

Doc Bar as a 5-year-old

"They thought he was beautiful!" smiled Stephenie, referring to her parents' infatuation with Doc Bar. "They had really never planned on buying a stallion, but their broodmare band grew and he was just so different."

The idea of owning a stallion, however, germinated slowly in their minds. Jasmine's desire for newborn foals to frolic in the pastures dominated the plans for the future of the Double J Ranch, thus inaugurating their purchase of broodmares. It seemed only normal then, that the purchase of a ranch-owned stallion should followed suit. Therefore, by the time Doc Bar sparked interest on the halter circuit, the Jensens, who relied heavily on Araujo's expertise to purchase their own show horses and build a broodmare band, were ripe to purchase a stallion.

Thea Jensen's first encounter with Doc Bar, however, left the youth with hesitant emotions about Mom and Dad purchasing him.

"My folks suggested that I ride Doc Bar around and see if I liked him, when we were at a horse show in Sacramento at the fairgrounds. It was not fun!" said Thea, but laughing now at the memory. "We were on the race track and Charley Araujo was holding him when I got on him. All he wanted to do though was run! I guess that track brought back memories to him."

Still, everyone agreed, he was a wonderful horse, handsome, and, when not on the race track with a young girl on his back, well behaved. Doc Bar was the one they wanted.

## Buying Doc Bar:

The stallion, still owned by Finley Ranch, could be bought with the right kind of deal. Araujo had already discussed with his good friend Marten Clark the possibility of Clark purchasing Doc Bar, but Clark, after considering the proposal, decided against buying him.

About the time that Clark rejected the proposal, the Jensens approached Araujo about purchasing Doc Bar.

"Charley did it," acknowledged Tom Finley, quick to praise the trainer for his ability to put an unusual sale together. "We wanted $30,000 for the stallion, but we didn't want money. We wanted that $30,000 in mares instead of dollars."

As soon as the Jensens agreed to the price and the purchasing method, the Finleys began the search for the right mares to add to their broodmare band.

"We knew exactly the type of mares that we wanted," recalled Finley. "We were looking for athletic ones to cross on Texas Dandy or Bob Charge, a Depth Charge stallion we were also standing at the ranch by then. It took about three months to find them all. We found some in California, some in Oklahoma, but none in Arizona. We got a mare by Leo, one by Depth Charge, another by Clabber II and one other mare. Some of the mares had records while some didn't, but they were all athletic.

Photo by Ed Ellinger.
Doc Bar shown by Doc Jensen.

"We also reserved two breedings to Doc Bar with the sale," continued Finley, "and wrote that on the back of the transfer.

With the new mares relocated to the Finley Ranch, the names of the owners on 6-year-old Doc Bar's registration papers changed for the first time and the sale was completed. Usually horses change ownership several times over the span of their lives, but the sale of Doc Bar to the Jensens would be the only change of ownership the stallion would ever have.

For Doc Bar himself, however, nothing changed. He remained, as he had since the day Charley Araujo brought him home from Tucson, Arizona, at the Araujo Ranch in Coalinga, California.

## Doc Bar Retires:

Doc Bar's halter winnings continued, but the show held October 19, 1962 at the Cow Palace in San Francisco, California, escalated him to the very height of his halter show career. The show, in the beginning, was like any other Quarter Horse Show. When the final scores were marked, however, Doc Bar and his get had swept the show. The stallion stood Grand Champion Stallion, but that was just the beginning for the Doc Bar family. His son, Barlet, the 1960 colt out of Nevada Starlet by Nevada King, was named Reserve Champion Stallion while his daughter, Janie Bar, a 1960 filly out of Red Jane C by King, was Reserve Champion Mare.

The final star added to Doc Bar's growing crown was winner of the Get-of-Sire class. This award at the show left little doubt of Doc Bar's ability to sire outstanding offspring. That year also began a six-year winning streak of the Get-Of-Sire class for Doc Bar.

Lee Berwick, who judged the Cow Palace show and who at one time had considered buying Doc Bar from Tom Finley, had no idea what the breeding of the horses was that he was placing, but he knew they had a new style.

"I never had seen any offspring of Doc Bar before, but at that show I made several of his offspring class winners. That was strange country to me and I'd never seen any of his foals before, but I just kept going to them for class winners and champions.

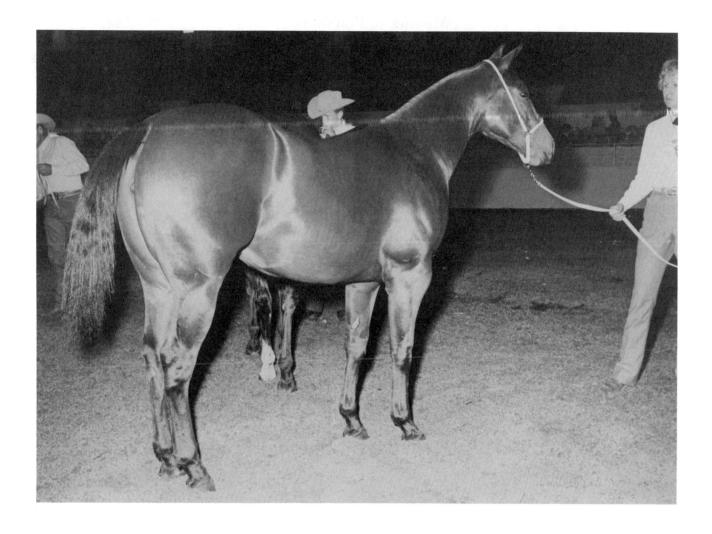

Jasmine Jensen showing an unidentified offspring of Doc Bar at halter.

"When I found out who the sire was I was pleasingly surprised. They were beautiful horses with lots of class."

Mare owners who had eyed the handsome stallion suspiciously with his early wins began considering Doc Bar genes for their mare's offspring and 12 mares attended the court of Doc Bar in 1962.

The glorious day was unequaled. Araujo, adhering to his creed to retire a horse from the arena when it achieved Grand Champion, advised the Jensens to do so. Doc Bar left the arena that day for the last time to bask not only in his own laurels, having accumulated 36 halter points, but to also bask in the laurels of his offspring.

The 1963 stud fee was also raised from $250 to $300.

## Moving to Paicines:

Enjoying the tranquility of the country and escaping the responsibilities of business topped the list of reasons for the Jensens to purchase the Double J Ranch. Since they were not interested in turning the ranch into a breeding operation, at the time of the purchase of Doc Bar, the couple left him in the capable hands of Araujo, preferring to take their mares to Doc Bar rather than bring him home and burden free weekends with breeding duties.

In reality, however, that intention also lacked the freedom they coveted. The purchase of Doc Bar played havoc with their freedom. To bring him home meant the responsibility of a breeding business at the ranch, a responsibility which they did not want. To carry their ever growing broodmare band to Doc Bar as each mare came in season, however, robbed them of precious free time as they spent weekend after weekend trailering mares to Coalinga.

What first seemed to be minor weekend excursions soon grew into major weekend pilgrimages. Instead of sipping coffee in the early Saturday morning hours while watching the changing colors of the surrounding mountains, Stephen Jensen hooked up the van in which they hauled horses, loaded a mare or two and began the long trek to Coalinga, the journey swallowing his precious weekend hours. Likewise, Jasmine, instead of riding horses along the river, joined her husband on the continuous journeys to Coalinga.

"Just to get to the ranch from Orinda was over a two-hour trip, so they would get there late Friday evening. Then early Saturday morning, they loaded broodmares and drove several hours to Coalinga, finally returning back to the ranch on Saturday night. That left little time on Sunday to spend at the ranch since it was back to Orinda on Sunday afternoon," explained Stephenie.

What was to be a week-end showplace was turning into an albatross around their neck. Trucking horses across California to be bred had not been a part of the dream.

In addition to the travel, since Doc Bar stood in Coalinga, the new foals that Jasmine Jensen envisioned around the ranch home, were always in Coalinga also while their mothers were being bred.

The decision was made. Doc Bar moved to Paicines at the end of the 1964 breeding season.

"They did try to stand him away from the ranch one other time," remembered Stephenie "At first they hired a breeder for the ranch, but that didn't work out so they sent Doc Bar over to Pleasanton to Dr. Goodbury's one year. Unfortunately, it really rained in California that year and since Dr. Goodbury's place was in a little canyon, that quickly filled with water. That didn't work out either."

Once again, Doc Bar was brought home, this time to stay. No more would they trailer their own mares to their own stallion standing on someone else's ranch. No more would Jasmine miss the freshness of new-born colts frolicking outside her windows. Stephen Jensen built Doc Bar his own personal bachelor barn with two large stalls and an adjoining pen and the couple proudly dubbed it "Doc's Barn."

An advertisement for Doc Bar, after listing his accomplishments, ended with an appropriate quotation: "Prepotency: a marked capacity on the part of an individual to transmit characters to the offspring, irrespective of the other member of the cross." Webster. It described Doc Bar well.

Before long, new help moved to Paicines, California.

# 8

## *Those Great Poco Tivio Daughters*

*After a while, you just run out of names. There were only so many times "Doc" or "Bar" mixed with a mare's name for something suitable to christen a colt. The entire Jensen clan tried to be creative, but with so many colts to name, after only a few years, the matter became a tedious one.*

*Finally, one day while discussing the lingering California drought, an idea dawned on Jasmine Jensen for a way to name the colts. Why not name them after something in particular, like the weather? Then, whenever they were discussing an offspring, it would be easy to know which other colts were born that same year.*

*From then on, naming colts became easy. Besides the year of weather, there was the year of nursery rhymes, the year of trees, the year of wines, the year of animals, the year of fish....*

\*\*\*

About the same time that Fizzabar captured the eyes of cutters, Janie Bar, also by Doc Bar and out of Red Jane C by King, who had already done well in halter competition, made attention-getting performances as a hackamore horse as well. The mare was a full sister to Poco Bueno, the sire of Poco Tivio. Teresa Tivio, the dam of Fizzabar was also by Poco Tivio. In fact, Poco Tivio mares, crossed on Doc Bar, produced some of the most outstanding performance horses.

When Fizzabar made her reputation," remembered Stephenie Ward, "my folks already had four or five daughters of Poco Tivio. A lot of people think it was the Poco Tivio daughters that were the best, but we also had good cutting horses out of a lot of other good mares. Our owning so many Poco Tivio mares, though, encouraged that thinking."

A few of the more influential mares that stood in the Jensen's pastures were Jameen Tivio, Lura Tivio, Teresa Tivio, Isla Tivio, Tasa Tivio and Susie's Bay.

## Jameen Tivio:

Ed Burgson of Sonora, California, bred the mare Jameen to Poco Tivio. The resulting foal was Jameen Tivio, who was purchased in 1959 by the Jensens from Charley Araujo. She became the first of six Poco Tivio mares that the Jensens eventually owned. A mare shown in halter by Charley Araujo when the Jensens bought her, Jameen Tivio had more of a career than halter shows and Doc Bar foals. The mare went to school.

"I took her with me to the boarding school that I attended during my high school years in Arizona," admitted Thea Jensen Essenger. "It was a big cattle ranch where we could bring our own horses and she went with me."

By the time the pair attended school, Thea had been riding and showing Jameen Tivio for some time. The Jensens had, in fact, purchased the mare with their daughter in mind.

"They thought she would be wonderful for me to show in stock-seat equitation since she really was a pretty, little horse. Jameen and I went to George Rose's in Hollister, California, and spent a good part of one summer there with him and his wife learning to ride. Since I had been riding Jameen that summer, she was just considered my horse, so off we went to school together."

Although Jameen Tivio theoretically became Thea's horse for awhile, the mare wasn't her favorite horse companion throughout the years. The mare, who would later produce outstanding offspring, had neither a pleasing personality nor a pleasing ride.

"She was the hardest horse to sit! She was short in the front end, the typical old Poco Tivio-style and I'd just cringe at the horse shows because I felt like I was bouncing a mile out of the saddle when it was suppose to look like a comfortable ride."

In addition to the rough ride, Jameen Tivio often displayed her sour personality and preferred nasty housekeeping habits in her stall, an aggravation to the young teenager since there were more important things to do than clean stalls. Thea, therefore, was not heart-broken when Jameen Tivio returned to the Double J Ranch.

Yet, no matter how rough she cantered or how bad she backed her ears, the mare excelled as a broodmare. She foaled seven colts between 1964 and 1973, four of them NCHA money earners and one, Doc's Lynx, an NCHA Futurity finalist and NCHA Derby Champion:

Doc's Cup Cake (1964); Doc's Hotrodder (1965) $389.62 NCHA money; Doc's Vanquero (1967); Doc's Lynx (1969) $9,866.09, Futurity Finalist, Derby Champion; Doc's Amador (1971); Doc's Tom Thumb (1972) $81.23, and Doc's Prescription (1973) $106.95.

## Lura Tivio:

Lura Tivio, out of Dottie Dee and by Poco Tivio, is most noted for her first foal, Doc's Dee Bar.

"After she was placed in the broodmare band, Charley Araujo brought her out to show in halter at the Cow Palace one year and she won Grand Champion," remembered Don Avila, the trainer who became synonymous with Doc's Dee Bar. "She was a big stout mare, a pretty mare with a nice head and neck. Of course, Charley Araujo believed in retiring a horse after it won Grand Champion, so she never returned to the ring"

Lura Tivio was bred accidentally one night when Doc Bar got out of his stall. At the time, the mare was only two years old and was destined for the show ring rather than the broodmare band. She foaled three colts, one of which, Doc's Dee Bar became a renowned reined cow horse:

Doc's Dee Bar (1963); Doc's Takla (1969), and Doc's Fri Dee Bar (1975).

## Susie's Bay:

"My folks bought Susie's Bay and actually had a trainer show her in the working cow horse event, but it just wasn't meant to be," said Stephenie. "First, she had been injured as a yearling and then later, when she was in training, she fell with the trainer and broke his leg two separate times! They decided not to show her anymore."

Susie's Bay, a 1955 mare out of Susie L by Poco Tivio, had eight colts from 1964 through 1974. From her union with Doc Bar, Doc's Marmoset was co-Champion of the NCHA Futurity while Doc's Oak placed in the NCHA Hall of Fame:

Doc's Susie Que (1964); Janey Durante (1965); Doc's Sweet Sue (1966), $321.32; Doc's Bar Bender (1967); Doc's Marmoset (1970), NCHA Silver Award; NCHA Futurity Co-Champion; Doc's Solano (1971); Doc's Oak (1973) $70,997.95, NCHA Hall Of Fame, NCHA Top Ten; NCHA Futurity Finalist, and Doc's Susie Bay (1974)

## Tasa Tivio:

Tasa Tivio, out of Chowchilla Pee Wee by Poco Tivio, lived on the Jensen Ranch until she died at the age of 26. One of the Jensens' favorite mares, Tasa Tivio was more like a pet than a broodmare. From 1965 until 1967 she had nine foals. Doc's Starlight, who was twice Reserve World Champion, was placed in the NCHA Hall of Fame while Doc's Topi and Doc Jensen were NCHA Futurity finalists:

Doc's Sly Guy (1965); Doc's Tassajara (1966), $34,877, NCHA Bronze Award; Doc's Starlight (1968), $134,442.30; NCHA Hall of Fame; NCHA Top Ten and two-time NCHA Reserve World Champion; Doc's Tlingit (1969) $23,144.36, NCHA Certificate of Ability; Doc's Topi (1970), $1,773.72, NCHA Futurity finalist; Doc Be Nimble (1972), $2,480.70, NCHA Certificate of Ability; Doc's Catalpa (1973); Doc's Muscat (1974) and Doc Jensen (1977), $16,204; NCHA Futurity finalist; NCHA Certificate of Ability

## Teresa Tivio:

Teresa Tivio, a mare whose get by Doc Bar blessed the performance industry with athletic horses, was never shown herself. The mare, out of Saylor's Little Sue by Poco Tivio, was described by Don Dodge, who had leased the mare and had owned at the time of Teresa Tivio's birth, as "a silly little thing." Although a producer of quality offspring, her disposition never improved.

"She was a good mare, but crazy," stated Stephenie. "She could be standing flatfooted and relaxed and all of a sudden go beserk. She would just self-destruct for no reason at all. Although Teresa Tivio was owned by Al Dolcini, she spent years at the Doc Bar Ranch in a trade-out breeding program in which

Doc Bar's racing career was short lived, winning only a meager $95; however, in the 1960's, Doc Bar and his offspring altered the guidelines for halter horse champions.

Doc Bar shown during his younger years. These photos were taken in the late 1960's by the Jensens.

## POCO LENA

While Doc Bar was establishing his prominence in the halter world, Poco Lena was racking up halter and cutting titles such as AQHA High Point Cutting Horse and NCHA World Champion Cutting Mare. During her lifetime, she achieved 184 halter points and 676 performance points.

Since she had been foundered badly, it was a miracle when she got in foal to Doc Bar. The resulting foal was Doc O'Lena, born June 21, 1967. The following year she foaled her second and last colt, Dry Doc, also sired by Doc Bar. Both offspring went on to win the prestigious NCHA Futurity.

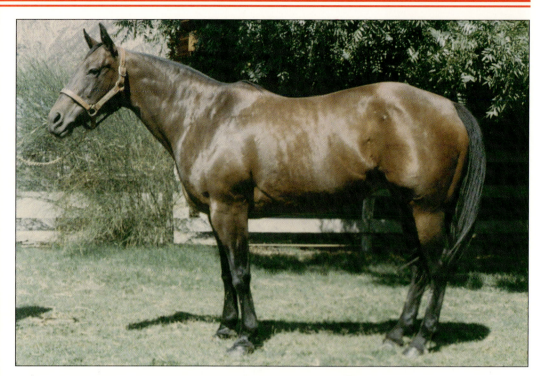

Poco Lena shown in July of 1965.

Poco Lena shown with Dry Doc. Since Poco Lena had been badly foundered, she spent a lot of time lying down.

Photo by Jasmine Jensen

Poco Lena shown with her 1968 foal, Dry Doc.

Doc O'Lena shown as a yearling.

Dry Doc shown after he was purchased by the King Ranch. At the lead shank is Joe Stiles.

Doc's Susie Que, a Doc Bar daughter out of Susie's Bay by Poco Tivio, shown as a yearling by Jasmine Jensen.

Another one of Doc Bar's great sons, Doc's Hotrodder, shown as a yearling in 1966.

Susie's Bay, an own daughter of Poco Tivio, with her one-day old filly, Doc's Marmoset. This photo was taken in March of 1970. This filly grew up to be the 1981 NCHA World Champion Cutting Horse, then owned by Bobby Condie, Salt Lake City, Utah, ridden by Tom Lyons. Susie's Bay was also the dam of Lyons' great cutting horse sire, Doc's Oak.

Doc Bar was purchased from the Finley Ranch by Stephen and Jasmine Jensen in 1962, when the stallion was a 6-year-old. That would be the final and only time there would be a transfer on the great stallion's AQHA papers.

Jasmine Jensen shown riding Doc Bar in December of 1966.

Stephen and Jasmine Jensen at their home in Orinda, California. This photo was taken in December of 1964.

Charlie Ward, a son-in-law to the Jensens, shown with Doc's Starlight, one of the greatest daughters of Doc Bar. This photo was taken in 1971 when the mare was a 3-year-old.

Charlie Ward showing Doc's Starlight, the great mare that went on to become Reserve World Champion Cutting Horse in 1977 and 1978 and World Champion Mare in 1977. She also finished in fifth place in 1975.

Charlie Ward shown in 1991 with Doc Bar (right) and "the new kid on the block," Grays Starlight. Grays Starlight, which is fast becoming a great sire himself, is sired by Peppy San Badger and out of Doc's Starlight.

Doc Bar shown in March of 1977 at the age of 21 at his home in Paicines, California.

Photo by David Brown

Even though Doc Bar could no longer breed mares, he was still in good shape at the ripe old age of 34.

## DON DODGE

Don Dodge, one of the greatest horsemen of his time, also owned and trained Fizzabar, a daughter of Doc Bar that was in the NCHA Top 10 for six years and was named World Champion Cutting mare in 1968. He also owned Poco Lena, the greatest daughter of Poco Bueno, that was in the NCHA Top 10 standings 10 times. She was the dam of Dry Doc and Doc O'Lena, both NCHA Futurity champions sired by Doc Bar.

Don Dodge played an important role in the life of Doc Bar. In 1951, he owned Poco Tivio, the great stallion whose offspring seemed to be the "magic cross" with Doc Bar. Dodge sold the stallion in 1952 to Charley Araujo.

Don Dodge's training facility in 1995.

## THE DOC BAR RANCH TODAY

The entrance to the Doc Bar Ranch located in Paicines, California. Today the ranch is run by Charlie and Stephenie Ward.

Mares grazing at the beautiful Doc Bar Ranch in Paicines, California.

Mares and colts still gather close to the grave of Doc Bar on the Doc Bar Ranch.

Doc Bar's grave is covered with flowers that Stephenie Ward keeps up year round.

Dr. Jensen and Dolcini engaged.

"Dad would breed someone else's mare and get the first colt; then he would breed her again and the owner would get the second colt That is how we got Doc's Haida."

Teresa Tivio had 10 colts. Doc's Haida, Doc's Remedy and Nu Bar were Futurity finalists while Fizzabar was inducted into the Hall of Fame:

Fizzabar (1961), NCHA Top Ten; NCHA Hall of Fame; Cattabar (1962); Cuttabar (1965); Cal Bar (1966), $10,426.84; NCHA Bronze; NCHA Top Ten; Cran Bar (1967), $728.45, NCHA Certificate of Ability; Doc's Haida (1969), $67,305.72, NCHA Futurity finalist, NCHA Bronze Award; Nu Bar (1970), $16,539.08, NCHA Futurity finalist, NCHA Derby finalist, NCHA Bronze Award; Boon Bar (1972), $12,325.19, NCHA Certificate of Ability; NCHA Futurity semifinals, NCHA Derby finalist; Doc's Remedy (1973), $47,453.10, NCHA Silver Award, NCHA Futurity finalist, NCHA Derby finalist; Doc Bar Gem (1975), $8,683.78, NCHA Certificate of Ability.

## Isla Tivio:

Isla Tivio out of Jimmette and by Poco Tivio, had unusual markings for the Poco Tivio bloodline, since she had a big white streak in her face.

"She was one that would definitely pass her heritage on," stated Stephenie. "Besides the streak, she would also have blue-eyed colts; we just never knew if we were going to get a baby that had one blue eye or two blue eyes. Between 1969 and 1974, Isla Tivio had six foals:

Doc's Kitwanga (1969); Doc's Wombat (1970); Doc's Inyo (1971), $2,847.54; Doc's Blue Eyes (1973); Doc's Malbec (1974); Docs Acey Deucey (1975).

These records, however, reflect only part of the story of the magical cross. Many of the get were shown in the American Quarter Horse Shows rather than in the National Cutting Horse Association where they and then their progeny excelled. An example is Doc's Prescription, which only won $106.95 in NCHA cutting competition, but in AQHA classes was shown 20 times in halter and won 18 of them. In addition, he won Grand Champion four times and Reserve Grand Champion seven times. The stallion sired 1,888 colts, of which 169 were open point earners, acquiring 3,685 open show points.

Interestingly, most all of the Poco Tivio mares owned by the Jensens did not have records, yet their foals became exceptionally well known. The Jensen clan believed that the trainability of a horse came from the dam's side, while the athletic ability came from the sire's side. As the get of the cross matured to show age and began sweeping the cutting horse industry, owners looked hard at the winning "Poco Tivio mare/Doc Bar cross," especially those Poco Tivio mares at the Jensen Ranch.

Isla Tivio, one of those great Poco Tivio mares, shown with a foal. Isla Tivio produced six foals by Doc Bar, including Doc's Wombat, Docs Acey Deucey and Doc's Malbec.

# 9

## *The Wards*

> *... The uniqueness of cutting remains undiluted. Like all great sports, you never get to the bottom of this one. Every horse is different, every rider is different, every cow is different. Seemingly invincible trainers go into sudden decline. Great horses quit or run off. Unknowns become famous in two and one-half minutes.*
>
> *Cutting is not show business or entertainment and its audience must make a serious attempt to understand it to enjoy it. Cutting is an extraordinary strenuous attempt by man to understand the horse in the context of work.*
>
> > *The Cutting Horse,*
> > *Forward by Tom McGuane,*
> > *National Cutting Horse Association,*
> > *1990.*

\*\*\*

For the most part Charlie and Stephenie Ward had spent their early married years on the rodeo circuit. Charlie, who rodeoed before they married, continued to do so after sharing his marriage vows with Stephenie Jensen, a daughter of Steve and Jasmine Jensen. Yet, both of them agreed that living on the road, traveling from one rodeo to another, was not a lifestyle they wanted to continue forever.

One wintry day while passing away the hours in their camper-living quarters while at the El Paso (Texas) Livestock Show and Rodeo, the couple discussed what type of work Charlie might pursue should they come off the road.

"You know, Steph," contemplated Charlie. "I've always wanted to ride a cuttin' horse; I think that might be a real money-maker! The other day when I was looking through a magazine, I saw an ad where a guy named Buster Welch is holding a cutting school before long; only thing is, it costs $500 to go."

The two discussed cutting horses for a while longer, getting more excited about the idea as the afternoon passed on. Charlie, remembering that a cutting was being held at the nearby rodeo grounds, suggested he and Stephenie drive down and see if this Mr. Welch might possibly be there.

As the couple walking among the stalls looking for someone to talk with, Charlie pointed toward a youngster tending to horses at the end of the barn. "Let's ask that skinny kid with those glasses on over there if he knows Mr. Welch."

Young Jimmy Bush, who was pouring grain into feed buckets, looked up over his glasses as Charlie Ward addressed him.

"Say kid, do you know a man named Buster Welch?"

"Sure do," grinned Jimmy, proudly. Then, assuming the conversation was over since everyone knew Buster Welch, he turned back to his chores."

Charlie sighed, shifted his weight from one foot to the other and rather disgruntled, continued, "Well, where do I find him?"

"Oh," acknowledged Jimmy, finally realizing this man did not know Buster Welch. "He'll be back here this evenin'. He's gonna show tonight."

With that tidbit of information, Charlie and Stephenie, excited about the prospect of seeing Buster Welch, decided to stay for the evening performance. Since the man was going to be putting on a school, Charlie felt certain that he would be putting on a show in the cutting arena that night. He, for one, did not want to miss it!

Charlie, an ace at roping but a greenhorn at cutting, was completely puzzled, however, when Welch's run ended. The man who everyone told him was an excellent cutter, the man who Charlie had already made his mentor, had only scored a 62. Dejectedly, he leaned over to Stephenie and whispered, "Maybe I should find the guy who wins this class and see if he's puttin' on a school!"

It didn't take long for Charlie Ward to learn that a cutting champion was a hero for that day only; the dawning of a new day could easily bring a new champ and hence a new hero. With this new perspective, Charlie was intrigued even more with this sport with numerous facets and before long, he checked in at the Welch Ranch, an eager student for a Buster Welch cutting school.

"All I had to ride was my rope horse and a two-year-old Doc Bar colt that we'd been leading in halter classes, but I knew so little about cuttin' that I figured they'd do, so I took them along. Buster, though, immediately took both of 'em away from me and gave me this other horse.

"Well, I threw my saddle on my school cuttin' horse and when I cinched him up, he tried to fall over on me. It was quite a way to start a school, but by the time it was all over, I'd had a really good time and met a bunch of good people."

He also left the school with a newly acquired addiction to cutting.

With cutting in his blood and with his in-laws, the Jensens, with a pasture full of horses, Charlie naturally began trying the sport on the available Doc Bar line. The next year he once again returned to a Welch School, this time with a Doc Bar colt that he had personally working on cattle.

By the time the school was over, another cutter, Mel Chartier, had partnered with several other cowboys and loaded Charlie's Doc Bar colt in their trailer and headed north. Charlie, with an empty trailer but a pocket full of money, headed west.

While Charlie Ward was learning about the thrills of cutting, the Jensens were tiring under the burdens of breeding.

"Mom and Dad had reached a point of exhaustion from trying to do all that they were doing. Their original plans to use the ranch as a play thing had gotten completely away from them," said Stephenie.

Besides needing help with their breeding program, the Jensens, who also had 12-15 head of 2-year-olds, by then needed the colts broke and started in training. Their son-in-law, Charlie Ward, seemed just the man for the job. Therefore, on January 1, 1969, Stephenie, Charlie, their 5-year-old son, Breon, and their three-month-old daughter, Tessa, moved to Paicines.

"It was a real relief for them when we moved down here. They could go back to enjoying the ranch when they came on the weekends rather than having all of these chores that had to be done. Back then, almost all of this place was in alfalfa and harvesting it alone was a major job.

Charlie Ward had more harvesting to do than just hay, however. Someone had to take over the breeding program and since one of his first jobs as a youngster was on a breeding farm, he was dutifully elected.

"I knew enough to know that I really didn't want to do the breeding, but we had let the breeding manager go, so I inherited the job," said Charlie, smiling wryly.

While breeding was never a favorite chore for Charlie, Stephenie settled into the routine and enjoyed the work. "I liked the breeding and working with the vet, but Charlie wasn't really interested in it. By that time he was hooked on cutting and wanted to do some training. Because of the breeding hours, though, he never got to go far from home. In fact. for six months every year, we had to be on the ranch daily."

Charlie and Stephenie brought the cutting fever to the ranch which readily fused easily into the non-halter-type mares that the Jensens had purchased. Slowly, interest in halter horses faded from the Double J Ranch. Just like Charley Araujo's interest in halter carried Doc Bar to halter championships, Charlie Ward's interest in cutting would, unknown to Charlie, carry champion Doc Bar blood into the cutting arena.

The jump from halter to cutting had been tempered by the kind of horses that the Jensens had purchased for their broodmares. Instead of purchasing halter-bred mares to breed to Doc Bar, they broke from tradition and purchased several Poco Tivio, King, Leo and Hollywood Gold daughters.

As he had from the Jensen's first step into the horse world, the friendship of Charley Araujo played a part in some of these purchases, but so did the desires of the Jensens to own horses that could "do something." The prominent couple, quite active on the Quarter Horse circuit, surprised equine followers with their choice of mares and reaped substantial criticism from doing so.

"Charley Araujo did not think that Doc Bar was athletic," said Stephenie. "The mares he had been breeding to Doc Bar had definitely been the halter-type horses, but my folks wanted horses that you could ride rather than just lead around. Therefore, they concentrated more on working lines."

The concentration proved to be a strong link for Doc Bar. With working line mares and Charlie Ward's interest in cutting, it was only a matter of time before Doc Bar get was introduced to cutting horse trainers.

Charlie continued to follow in the footsteps of Buster Welch. At that time, another cowboy, Shorty Freeman, also worked at the Welch Ranch. The two struggling, young trainers, conscious of the need of good horseflesh to win prizemoney at cuttings, took a long, hard look at the new style of horse Ward brought from California to the Welch schools in West Texas. In fact, they knew about two horses by Doc Bar, Fizzabar and Janie Bar, who had already made waves in the competition world.

The Poco Tivio influence has been so great in making Doc Bar famous. This is a snapshot taken of Charlie Ward holding Poco Tivio when the stallion was 25 years old.

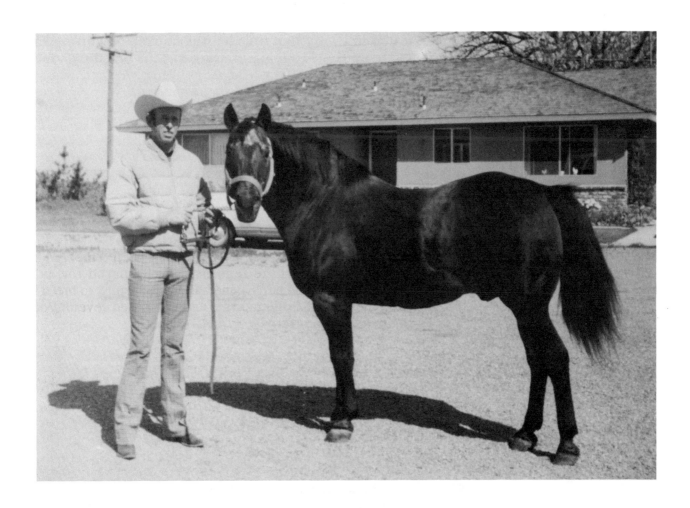

With Buster and Shorty being hungry, talented and always eager to try the unknown, the Doc Bar get interested them. It would be only a few short years before Doc Bar offspring would partner with both of these trainers for the biggest prize money of all, and the unknown stallion would immediately become famous.

At the same time, it was a changing era in the halter world as well. While the Jensens concentrated on working lines rather than halter lines, the Quarter Horse industry slowly moved toward another style of horse. In halter, Doc Bar offspring were receiving fewer and fewer blue ribbons.

Yet, Doc Bar, through his offspring and his new promoter, had begun his own transition, leaving behind the quiet world of correct stance, glistening coats and a trainer at the shank. They had moved on to the active world of eye-to-eye combat and rapid-fire movements in the performance world.

# 10

## *Fizzabar*

*Most of the battles of life are won*
*by looking beyond the clouds to the sun*
*And having the patience to wait for the day*
*When the sun comes out and the clouds float away!*

Helen Steiner Rice

\*\*\*

Although Doc Bar and his get established quite a winning streak in the halter classes for a while, the stallion was unable to transform the halter image completely. Neither could his transformation remain year after year. Just as Doc Bar had changed the conformation style among halter winners from heavier-bodied horses to his more-refined body style, with time the industry again shifted, this time away from the Doc Bar image.

"I don't think the Doc Bar horses were big enough for the halter people," offered Marten Clark. "I don't believe they had enough size to them, so people quit breeding for them."

For whatever reason, Doc Bar, once a prominent breeder for halter get, had several years where few outside mares visited his court. A complete career exchange, however, lay just beyond the horizon for him, initiated by one of his offspring, Fizzabar, a 1961 mare by Doc Bar and out of Teresa Tivio.

Fizzabar provided the first indication of the impact that the progeny of Poco Tivio mares crossed on Doc Bar would have on cutting. Yet, the road to the cutting arena was long and arduous.

"Harry Rose started Fizzabar and showed her as a

3-year-old in hackamore classes, which were similar to the working cow-horse classes of today," remembered Don Dodge.

The mare, with Rose riding her, made quite an impression in the hackamore competition. She had both the ability and the looks to attract attention.

"The first time I remember seeing Fizzabar, Harry Rose showed her in the reined cow horse classes," stated cutting horse trainer Stanley Bush of Mason, Texas. "I thought she was one of the nicest little mares in the business. She was a dainty little thing with the cutest little head; you couldn't help but notice her!"

After Rose showed Fizzabar extensively, Arnold Dolcini, the owner of Fizzabar, decided to consign her to the

Don Dodge astride Fizzabar

Cow Palace Horse Sale. Dodge, who rode horses for Chunky Woodward, agreed to bid on Fizzabar for the Woodwards since Mrs. Woodward wanted the horse.

"Chunky said he'd signal me if the bidding got too high," stated Dodge.

Trainer Jack Brainard, remembering that sale, applauded Harry Rose's ingenuity for demonstrating the mare to the crowd. "Harry, instead of riding Fizzabar himself, put his 10-year-old son, little Harry, on her. That mare did some fabulous things in that ring with a kid on her back, so naturally, that ran the price on up there."

After the gavel fell on Dodge's $7,500 bid under the watchful eye and agreeing nod of Woodward, Dodge hauled the mare home with him to his barn at 3400 El Paso Boulevard in Sacramento, California.

Dodge, besides being a notable hunter/jumper trainer, had also developed quite a reputation in all facets of the horse industry. In fact, the trainer had been instrumental in introducing the sport of cutting to California.

"Don Dodge had more horsemanship ability than any man I ever knew," commended Marten Clark. "He was quite a diverse individual. He could recite Shakespeare as well as train horses, and he trained some outstanding ones. He was probably one of the smartest showmen I ever saw."

Dodge's talents were tested, however, with Fizzabar, who, by the time she moved to Sacramento with her new trainer, had run the arena fence so many times, that her desire to work had dissipated.

"Harry showed Fizzabar hard; in fact, he'd just about burned her up," said Dodge, eyebrows knitted in concentration, hands clasped with fingers pointed against his lips. "You know, it's like every horse has a head full of marbles and little holes. Now, when the marbles fall out, you have trouble getting them back in the holes. That's the way it was with Fizzabar.

"She'd run those cows up and down the fence in the working cowhorse classes for so long, she wouldn't even look at one, much less cut one. And that's not all; you couldn't stop her either - she'd rear up - and she wouldn't back up! I didn't know what I'd gotten myself into."

Dodge, whose bleachers in his indoor arena were often spotted with spectators watching his training session, refused to allow anyone to stay and watch a training session with Fizzabar. Since she was a nervous mare, Dodge worked her daily for over a year before she ever noticed a cow. As Fizzabar began to show interest in her training program, though, Dodge, for the first time, felt that perhaps the mare was worthy of the $7,500 that Woodward had given for her.

Shortly after Fizzabar accepted her cutting training, Dodge's faith in the mare got tested. One day Chunky Woodward stopped by the barn to visit with his trainer and during their conversation, he admitted Mrs. Woodward seemed to have lost interest in Fizzabar. He suggested that Dodge sell her for $10,000.

For Don Dodge, it had been a long, tough year training Fizzabar, but one he did not want to throw away. The mare, who was definitely athletic, was developing a gleam in her eye about a cow; in fact, he felt her nervous energy might be channeling itself into a challenging spirit, a great asset for a cutting horse. He just felt the marbles were finally falling into place.

Although, Dodge didn't have $10,000, he had half of it, and he was willing to bet on Fizzabar for the other half. With $5,000 down and a promise to pay the remaining $5,000 by the end of the year, Don Dodge became the owner of Fizzabar.

"When the mare became mine, though," reminisced Dodge, "it seemed she automatically went from bad to worse. One morning, when I was thoroughly disgusted with her, Kenny Sutton came by. Angrily, I told him I thought I'd just give up on training her for cutting; I'd just bridle her and show her in the bridle class. But, Kenny didn't see things the way I did and he said, 'Tell ya what, you just keep after her and any time in the rest of that mare's life you want to sell her, I'll give you your $10,000 back for her.' That gave me a little incentive to keep on trying to train Fizzabar to cut!"

Sutton correctly perceived a winning trainer and a winning horse that just needed time to mold together. Within the year, Fizzabar and Dodge made great strides in the cutting arena so the trainer decided to carry his prize to the California State Fair.

"We were stabled in the back of the fair grounds at barn 24 with about 30 head of horses," chuckled Dodge, remembering the day. "I decided to ride Fizzabar around the place for a little experience and we were doing just fine until I went around a pole and a bunch of those white birds flew up.

"That did it. Away she went and I couldn't stop her! She was flying! She ran clear to the clubhouse-turn and almost back to the barn with everybody watching and me trying to stop her all the while. Needless to say, they laughed about that for years."

Although the incident remained fodder for laughter, Fizzabar did not. Instead, she adapted quickly in the sport of cutting, building a reputation as a tough competitor. Dodge's perseverance and hard work produced a top-notch contender in the cutting horse arena.

Stanley Bush, who traveled to shows with Dodge, remembered how the mare he had admired in the hackamore classes transformed into a mare with exceptional cutting talents.

"She was an athletic little bugger, a catty little mare. She wasn't ill-tempered and she wasn't hard to haul. I think she was probably one of the best of the Doc Bar mares."

By 1967, Fizzabar sat seventh in the National Cutting Horse Association Top Ten standings, having won $8,179.23. The pair returned to the Top Ten to earn fourth place in the standings with $11,868.90 in 1968, and that year they also took home the title of World Champion Cutting Mare. Again, in 1969, Dodge and Fizzabar earned seventh place in the standings, having accumulated $7,558.93 but when Fizzabar broke the Top Ten in 1970 in sixth place, with earnings of $6,625.50, she had a new trainer, Leon Harrel, on her back.

Three years later, in 1973, she ended the year in the NCHA Top Ten standings again, ridden by a third trainer, Gene Suiter of Oakdale, California. With $9,121.56 won that year, Fizzabar sat in seventh place, the last time she would enter the Top Ten standings.

Those were tough years of cutting. Fizzabar competed against horses such as Peppy San, Senor George, Chickasha Dan, Royal Chess, Jose Uno, King Skeet, and Gandy's Time. Her continual grit year after year, however, turned heads among the cutting population and made owners look at the pedigree of the spunky little reined cowhorse-turned-cutter. Surprising to many, her sire was an unknown stallion, a halter-winner named Doc Bar, which stood off the beaten path at Paicines, California.

# 11

## *Poco Lena Comes to Doc Bar*

*When Doc Bar was born in 1956, Poco Lena was already a princess in the cutting arena. When he went to the track in 1958, she had already been in the NCHA World Champion standings five times. In the early 60's when Doc Bar established his prominence in the halter world, she had racked up titles such as AQHA High Point Cutting Horse and NCHA world Champion cutting mare.*

*But when they came together at the Double J Ranch in 1966, Doc Bar made the princess a Queen; Poco Lena made the halter champ a King.*

\*\*\*

The California halter crowd knew about Doc Bar's uniqueness and the performance crowd was taking a second look at him, thanks to progeny such as Fizzabar and Janie Bar. It was a fabled mare foaled in 1949, however, one who had won almost $100,000 in 11 years of cutting during the time when a quarter would buy a hamburger, that catapulted his name into a household word in the cutting horse industry. Poco Lena, by Poco Bueno and out of Sheilwin, a full sister to Poco Tivio, foaled two colts by Doc Bar that set the cutting world on fire for Doc Bar progeny.

### Poco Lena: The Champion Cutting Mare

"I told Milt Bennett the year after we had hauled together that I'd decided to sell Poco Lena; I had some others coming on and I didn't think I needed her," reminisced Don Dodge. "I never will forget what he told me. He said, 'Don, you'll only be sorry once and that'll be from that day on.' You know, he was right."

From the first time Dodge saw Poco Lena, he knew that some day he had to own that mare. At the time, Andy Hensley, who broke horses on the Waggoner Ranch, rode her every day to his house on the ranch for lunch.

"He'd tie her up at noon and she'd dig a hole you could bury an elephant in while he was eatin' lunch," said Dodge. "She was a nervous type but she was just a plumb natural with cutting. The first time she saw a cow, she just splattered on that ground. The first time I rode her was at Waggoners when it was just Andy and me and none of those other people around!" laughed Dodge.

When she was ready to show, trainer Pine Johnson took Poco Lena to her first registered cutting in Dallas and won the class. At that time, Waggoner had given Snipper W to Johnson and he then gave Poco Lena to his ranch manager, from whom Dodge finally purchased the mare for $10,000.

Just as it was with Fizzabar, however, the road to success on Poco Lena tested Dodge's patience and ability.

"I didn't show my pride and joy a cow until I got her home to Sacramento. We rode horses outside in the open country back then, so I'm out there walking her around and I'm so proud of her. Everything's fine until I kick her into a lope and when I did, this mare took off like a raving idiot and boy can she run! She doesn't give up either!

"Back in those days, I used to smoke cigarettes and I smoked plenty of them because of her. I'd get so mad at her because I couldn't lope her. Day after day, it was the same thing. You'd think that after a while she'd change, but not her! This mare had heart! You'd get to fighting her and that was worse, so I'd get off of her, sit under a tree and just stare at her while smoking a cigarette and cussin' her."

Rather than persist with the feud, Dodge devised a compromising way to prepare Poco Lena for cuttings.

"We showed at a lot of rodeos back then. You'd be at those shows for a long time and there wasn't a lot of places to ride your horses since there was always a show going on. We'd all have to get up at 3 in the morning so we could get in the arena and get them ridden. I think half of those boys would get up and come down there just to watch me.

"It was the same thing every time. I'd take Poco Lena in the arena and we'd start out just gigging along for a little while. Then I'd stand up on her and let her run. Her belly would be almost on the ground as she went flying around that arena, running just as hard as she could. After a few laps of that, she'd start to slow down. Finally she'd stop and let out this huge deep breath, and then I'd know she was going to be ready for the cuttin'. I tell ya, me getting Poco Lena ready to show entertained a lot of people back then."

Although the battle raged between trainer and mare when out in the open country, the two worked like a fine-tuned clock in the cutting arena. The trainer gave the mare all of the credit.

"She had a lot of ability and whole lot of cow; she just didn't take any training," continued Dodge. "You just showed her the cow, moved her up a little, and she'd take care of the rest. We had re-run cattle; they'd bring about 45 in the arena and we'd work them every performance. You got to where you called everyone of them by name! Back in those days, a horse had to go get a cow and she could do it. I really thought a lot of her."

Dodge, however, did sell Poco Lena to non-professional rider B.A. Skipper, who wore a seat belt in the saddle to stay aboard during her quick moves and sharp turns. During her show career this phenomenal mare placed in the NCHA World Champion standings 10 times, when there was no separate class in which non professionals showed, earning $99,782.

Five times, Poco Lena earned the title of NCHA Reserve World Champion: in 1952 and 1953 with Dodge riding her, and in 1959, 1960 and 1961 with B.A. Skipper riding her. Three times she was World Champion Cutting Mare. Besides achieving the NCHA Silver Cutting Award and the Bronze Cutting Award, Poco Lena also earned her rightful place in the NCHA Hall of Fame.

In a tribute to the great mare in the April, 1963, NCHA <u>Cuttin' Hoss Chatter</u>, the author stated, "In 11 years, Poco Lena placed in 395 cutting horse contests approved by the National Cutting Horse Association and won a total of $99,782.13 in competition against all who challenged. This amount stands first in the all-time money winners in the history of our Association. In fitting recognition of this great lifetime performance, Poco Lena has been awarded Hall of Fame Certificate Number 1 by the National Cutting Horse Association and a plaque attesting to this honor will be hung in the home of the Association."

At the same time the mare was making a prestigious name for herself in the National Cutting Horse Association, she was doing the same in the American Quarter Horse Association, earning the title of AQHA High-Point Cutting Horse in 1959, 1960 and 1961. She achieved 184 halter points and 676 performance points.

Her record as NCHA all-time money earner no longer stands today. However, neither does a quarter buy a hamburger.

Poco Lena's show career came to an untimely end when her new owner, B. A. Skipper, was killed when his private plane crashed while he was flying home to Longview, Texas. He and Poco Lena had just won a cutting in Douglas, Arizona. The crash occurred in the early morning hours of October 1, 1962. The saddle he used to ride Poco Lena sits in memorial at the NCHA office today.

It took a while for Skipper's plane to be located and for him to be pronounced dead. During this time, Poco Lena, who was being trailered home along with another outstanding cutting horse, Holey Sox, was left in a horse trailer and not located until October 5. The five-day ordeal without food and water took its toll on both of the horses. Although Holey Sox was able to return to the cutting arena, Poco Lena, her feet already in poor condition, suffered extensive foundering and never cut again.

## Poco Lena Comes To Paicines

"Doc O'Lena and Dry Doc were miracles!" exclaimed long-time auctioneer Ike Hamilton, "Why, if Poco Lena had stayed in Louisiana, she'd probably never been bred to Doc Bar."

Hamilton, the auctioneer for the horses at the estate sale of B. A. Skipper, remembered well the sale held at the rodeo grounds at Gladewater, Texas, and the final negotiations that took Poco Lena to California rather than Louisiana. An overflowing crowd representing 40 states and Canada attended the March 20, 1963, dispersal.

"It seemed like every Quarter Horse man in the country was there at the sale," remembered Hamilton of Monroe, Louisiana. "Several of them even brought their vets to look at her because everybody knew about her condition. When we got to her in the sale, Milo Sullivan, who was sales manager, read this report on her. It was a long one that told all about her health.

"When the bidding finally started, quite a few bid on her at first. D.C. Johnston, who was standing behind me, was a heavy bidder and bid on her up to $14,000, but Grady Madden, stepped in then, bid $14,200 and bought her."

After the sale, while the mare was enroute to Minden, Louisiana, Madden decided to not consummate his purchase and Poco Lena was held at the Texas state line cattle rest for several days while B. A. Skipper's mother, who was in charge of his estate, and Mr. Madden attempted to settle their differences. Once again, left without proper care, Poco Lena's feet continued

Henley Photo
Poco Lena was NCHA World Champion Cutting Mare three times and Reserve World Champion five times. Besides achieving the NCHA Silver and Bronze awards, she also earned her place in the NCHA Hall of Fame.

to deteriorate. Once a cutting horse star, she now waited in a cattle pen, the object of rejection.

While the turmoil persisted in Texas, out in California, Bob Elliott, a good friend of the late B. A. Skipper, was visiting in the Jensen home. In their conversation, Jasmine Jensen, not knowing the Texas chaos, mentioned to Elliott that she would have liked to have purchased Poco Lena to breed to Doc Bar. Elliott, however, aware of the Poco Lena controversy, suggested the purchase might still be possible. At Mrs. Jensen's request, he negotiated with the parties involved and the Jensens purchased Poco Lena for $12,500.

Once the purchase was finalized, the entire Jensen clan elatedly awaited their new mare's arrival, which was being hauled to California in a special trailer equipped with foam-rubber floor boards to soften the ride. However, rather than the ranch being her first stop, it was in Salinas at the veterinarian clinic of Dr. Frank Wayland and Dr. Gary Deter. Their exuberance was short lived.

"When Poco Lena slowly hobbled off the trailer, everyone was just sick to see her physical condition," remembered Stephenie. "She was in such pain."

For several days, the Jensens debated whether to put Poco Lena down or try to save her. The mare, who once grittily challenged cows nose-to-nose with lightning-quick speed, could barely stand. Immediately they consulted with Dr. Frank Wayland, who gave them faith that Poco Lena might could be helped.

"At that time, we were dealing with the first radical resection of the toe with foundered horses," remembered Dr. Deter. "We attempted this with an acrylic foot, but we didn't have much success. We were just able to help her a little. She was a great old mare and she took care of herself. We had her on our irrigated pastures for a long time and she was on the ground 90 percent of the time. She really had a lot of heart."

Only a stone's throw away from the great mare, Doc Bar regally stood in his barn. Like so many other events in the life of Doc Bar, the rejection of Poco Lena, however, was serendipity for the stallion. Just as rejection from the race track had ultimately made the stallion famous in the halter industry, Poco Lena's unbelievable arrival to the court of Doc Bar would, in only a few short years, electrify the cutting horse industry with Doc Bar fever.

## The Fairy-Tale Foals

Wayland worked to not only improve the mare's feet, but to get her in foal. During her years of showing, Poco Lena had been medicated to stop her heat cycles, making conception difficult now. In addition, the mare was already 14 years old and had never had a foal.

"She had no ovulatory activity for almost two years," said Deter. "Any attempts we did to promote her to ovulate didn't work. Then, in 1966, she conceived. I was in total disbelief!"

Stephenie also remembered Dr. Wayland's surprise when the mare conceived. "We were all so excited. Even Dr. Wayland, who was in the hospital at the time, couldn't wait to get out so he could feel that the mare was in foal."

Marten Clark, a close friend of Dr. Wayland and Dr. Deter, praised the Jensens for taking the chance with Poco Lena and the veterinarians for their conscientious effort to assist the mare.

"Dr Wayland was a brilliant vet. He really worked with this mare; he ultimately removed the outer shell of the hooves and that helped her feet some. He literally saved the mare to the point that she could have two foals."

The front lawn of the Jensen home, with its lush grass and huge trees, provided a safe haven for a valuable mare which could barely walk, While other broodmares grazed in adjoining pastures, separated by a white board fence, Poco Lena hobbled around the Jensen yard. In only a short while, she curiously nibbled the thick shrubbery and before long devoured the clusters of flowers once accenting the lawn.

Graciously, Jasmine Jensen allowed Poco Lena, by then "Queen" of the ranch, to munch her flowers, nibble the shrubs and consume the lawn. Jasmine, so protective and soft-hearted with the mare, would even lay blankets across the rocky driveway to create an easier path for the mare to hobble. Often when Poco Lena laid down, Jasmine knelt beside her and rubbed her legs. The appearance of the ranch, the esthetic charm Jasmine always enjoyed, lost its importance. What was more important was that Poco Lena was finally in foal with her first Doc Bar offspring.

Doc O'Lena, the first miracle colt, was born June 21, 1967. "I went out to see him and I couldn't believe how tiny he was," exclaimed Deter. "Why, he could run under his mother's belly with his ears pricked, and never touch her."

Soon afterwards, the bottom rungs of the yard plank fence separating pasture and lawn were removed so that the young colt could slip into the pasture and frolic with other newborns. Poco Lena, laying on the lawn under the shade of a massive sprawling tree, watched her frisky first-born as he tested the waters of independence. Doc O'Lena, however, returned frequently to the front lawn where his dam, Poco Lena, stayed to receive the assurance and love only a mother could give.

The following year, when Doc O' Lena was a yearling, another colt, this one christened Dry Doc, was also born on the Jensen lawn. By that time, however, Poco Lena's degenerating health guaranteed Dry Doc would be her last foal. Soon after her second colt was weaned, Poco Lena, losing weight and continually in pain, was mercifully put down.

## The Doc Bar Explosion In The Cutting Industry

"Man, I really like your horse," commented Dennis Funderburgh as he rode past Shorty (Freeman) in the warm-up area of the Will Rogers coliseum. With confidence in his eyes and no swagger in his voice, Shorty glanced over at Funderburgh and quietly answered, 'You ain't seen nothing yet'" (Nettles, Gala. Just Shorty, Nettles Publishing, 1990)

True to his word, Freeman riding Doc O' Lena at the 1970 NCHA Futurity, brought the crowd to their feet with thunderous applause as the pair captured the 1970 NCHA Futurity Championship, setting a record as the only horse to ever win both go-rounds, the semi-finals and the finals - a record which still stands today.

Only the previous year, Freeman had won the title of NCHA Reserve Futurity Champion riding another Doc Bar offspring, Doc's Kitty out of Kitty Buck by Pretty Buck. Neither of them were the first Doc Bars to show in the NCHA Futurity, however, since trainer Bobby Ingersoll had taken Knotty Bar, a stallion out of Mansita by Jimmie Reed to the 1968 Futurity.

Knotty Bar was a real cowhorse," remembered Ingersoll. "He was a really intelligent-looking horse like his dad and easy to train. I made the second go-round on him and the owner, Lendell Gray, who owned Graywood Ranch got a lot of compliments on him. People wanted to know his breeding and if there were any more like him."

Ingersoll had shown another Doc Bar get, a 1962 foal out of Mansita, Doc's Doby Bar, on the Pacific Coast, winning numerous working cowhorse classes on the stallion. In fact, the year that Doc O' Lena won the 1970 NCHA Futurity, Doc Bar had already sired 206 foals. Most of them that were shown, however, were shown in halter classes.

Doc O'Lena, the first offspring out of Poco Lena by Doc Bar, won the 1970 NCHA Futurity. With Shorty Freeman in the saddle, the stallion set a record as the only horse to ever win both go-rounds, the semifinals and the finals - a record which still stands today.

While his halter record had enhanced his breedings in the early 60's, when the halter conformation once again took another turn, outside bookings for Doc Bar's stallion service waned for a while. By that time, however, the Jensens had established a strong set of broodmares, so Doc Bar babies were still steadily being born. The cutting horse industry, with its home-base in Fort Worth, Texas, was just learning of the California jewel.

All eyes were on Dry Doc, Doc O'Lena's full brother and the last son of Poco Lena, at the 1971 NCHA Futurity. Ridden by trainer Buster Welch, the pair did not disappoint the crowd. With Dry Doc's win of the coveted 1971 NCHA Futurity Championship, both Doc Bars sons out of the immortal Poco Lena, had been crowned consecutive "Kings" of the NCHA Futurity.

Dry Doc, Doc O'Lena's full brother and the last colt out of Poco Lena, was the 1971 NCHA Futurity Champion ridden by Buster Welch. The stallion is shown here with his owner Mel Chartier and his son Randy.

# 12

## *Prime Time*

A crisp fall morning abruptly greeted Charlie Ward as he walked out the front door of the house. Although much of the late fall foliage still clung stubbornly to the trees scattered throughout the valley, Charlie noticed an array of colorful leaves already haphazardly covered the path leading to the barn. Falling leaves were a definite notification that Old Man Winter was on its way.

Charlie made a mental note to make sure the horse blankets that were removed from the horses that morning were loaded into the trailer. He grinned to himself as memories of other futurities from previous years flooded his mind. There had been the time he had left sunny California only to pull his rig into a snow-covered coliseum parking lot two days later, and of course, he hadn't had blankets for the horses! One thing for sure, the unpredictable cold weather in Fort Worth, Texas, usually made the weather in Paicines look like spring.

Charlie walked straight to the trailer which had been loaded the night before with the necessary tack and feed for a trip that lasted almost a month. It was hard to remember everything for a trip like this; in fact, it was hard to even know for sure what he would need before he would pull back into the Doc Bar Ranch shortly before Christmas. "Let's see, yep, there were the horse blankets, saddle pads, bridles, saddles, brushes and even the medicine chest."

In only a short period of time, horses and suitcases were loaded in the trailer. Charlie settled himself behind the wheel of the truck, anxious to get on the road since many hours lay ahead before his first stop tonight. There was a chance, however, at tonight's stop that he might sell one of the two-year-old Doc Bar colts he had in the trailer.

*Instantly he slammed on the truck brakes. Horse papers and transfers! He had forgotten the horse papers and transfers.*

\*\*\*

It was almost like the California Gold Rush of 1849, instead, it was the sizzling seventies and the California Doc Bar rush. Like gold, however, Doc Bar, rather than being a new commodity, for awhile was just an overlooked asset on the West Coast.

Even though he was a new phenomenon to the cutting horse industry, Doc Bar was already 15 years old by the time Dry Doc won the 1971 NCHA Futurity. The Jensens, who by then had owned him almost ten years, had, however, faithfully bred their stallion to their own band of broodmares, unknowingly building a personal dynasty in cutting horses.

While the back-to-back NCHA Futurity championships of Doc O'Lena and Dry Doc electrified cutting horse people from the Atlantic to the Pacific Coast, the great horse, Gun Smoke's Dream, by capturing the title in 1972, interrupted the roll of consecutive Doc Bar offspring champions, but only for a year. Although a Doc Bar get did not win the coveted 1972 title, the sire was well represented in the Futurity Finals.

Doc's Tlell, by Doc Bar out of Gold Corrour by Hollywood Gold, earned fourth place. The gelding, owned by Kim Sullivan of Houston, Texas, was ridden by Sam Wilson. Three horses tied for fifth, sixth and seventh places and two of them, Doc's Lynx, owned and shown by Tom Lyons, and Doc's Nanaimo, owned and shown by Jim Lee, were own sons of Doc Bar. Charlie Ward showed Doc's Haida, owned by Dr. and Mrs. Jensen, to tie for top honors in the semifinals, but did not make the Finals cut. The Doc Bar lineage was definitely on a roll.

The prestigious title returned to Doc Bar progeny the next two years, however. Ridden by Tom Lyons, Doc's Marmoset, out of Susie's Bay by Poco Tivio, captured the title of the 1973 NCHA Futurity Champion while Doc's Yuba Lea, out of My Dinah Lea by Leo, won the 1974 NCHA Futurity with Leon Harrel aboard.

With four Doc Bar get winning Futurity championships in five years, the Doc Bar name literally reverberated whenever cutting dominated the conversations. Serious cutters pulled out their California maps and examined them carefully, searching for an obscure locale called Paicines.

All of a sudden, the quiet valley with which Jasmine and Stephen Jensen had fallen in love with almost 15 years earlier, their tranquil getaway from the pressures of professional life, buzzed with business. All four NCHA Futurity winners were out of Jensen mares, so the ranch telephone rang constantly, prospective buyers anxiously wanting the Jensens colts, believing they carried the miracle-genes to capture NCHA Futurity titles. Asphalt on the once quiet, winding road that led to the ranch, hummed with activity, a virtual freeway of horse trailers careening precariously around the mountainside, racing to own a part of the Doc Bar heritage.

In 1973, 38 Doc Bar foals were born followed by 43 live foals in 1974.

Once, in a discussion with several top stallion owners about breeding farms, Shorty Freeman quietly listened as the men listed requirement after requirement for a successful operation. Easy access to the facilities carried foremost importance. Freeman, whose name had become synonymous with Doc Bar's son, Doc O'Lena, since their famous Futurity grand slam, dropped his cigarette to the ground, mashed it with the toe of his boot and interrupted their conversation.

"There's not one bit of truth in that location-stuff, boys. Just look at Doc Bar! You almost can't get to him, but that hasn't stopped one owner that wanted to breed his mare to him from making the trip."

In 1975, Shorty Freeman returned once again to win the NCHA Futurity title, and once again he rode a horse with Doc Bar genes. The 1975 winner, Lenaette, out of Bar Sox Babe and owned by Terry Riddle, was, however, sired by Doc Bar's son, Doc O'Lena, and, therefore, the first grand-get of Doc Bar to become a Futurity Champion. Doc O' Lena also sired the 1976 NCHA Maturity winner, Lena's Peppy. These two champions especially excited an industry already at a frenzy for Doc Bar breeding, since their championships proved the potency of the Doc Bar line.

For every remaining year of the 1970s, a Doc Bar progeny made the winner's circle of the NCHA Futurity and Doc Bar fever ran rampant. Almost every foal born with a hint of Doc Bar blood in its veins carried the great sire's name. Time and again, they reaped more esteem upon the stallion.

## Back At The Ranch

During these dynamic Doc Bar years, the desire for Doc Bar progeny gained popularity so rapidly that the 70 maximum breeding contracts issued each year quickly vanished. Contracts arrived back in the ranch mail box as early as December for the first February breedings and by February or March, Doc Bar's' 'date book' overflowed.

"We never accepted more than 70 mares to breed to Doc Bar plus the four or five that we might have left over from the years before," stated Stephenie. "We figured that limiting the number of breedings would make the colts more valuable.

"Neither were we selective about the mares who came, although I tried to be once or twice. Instead, we thought one of the best ways to be selective would be to raise the stud fee."

Even when the fee reached $4,000, the flow of mare-owners desiring to breed to Doc Bar never ebbed. With each passing year, another group of colts reached show-age, with a majority of them winning in some class somewhere. The phenomenal record of Doc Bar's offspring increased the odds that buying a breeding to the great stallion would pay off in big bucks.

Dr. Gary Deter, the vet who had assisted Dr. Frank Wayland for years in taking care of the Jensens' horses, continued to assist Charlie and Stephenie with the Doc Bar breeding program after Dr. Wayland lost his battle to cancer. Unique to most other breeding farms, breeding on the Doc Bar Ranch depended on the weather since their vet usually flew to the ranch.

"One of the greatest pleasures of my life is to be a pilot and be in the vet business, also," admitted Deter. "I had a triangle that I flew for years when Doc Bar was breeding. I'd fly early in the morning to Marten Clark's ranch, then go from there to the Doc Bar Ranch. That would take the rest of the morning, and then Charlie's mom fixed us lunch. If possible, you always wanted to be around for her fabulous home cookin!"

Foggy weather in Salinas, where Deter practiced veterinarian medicine, meant a slow start in Paicines breeding mares. "He could easily be fogged in until 10 o'clock," remarked Stephenie. "Gary flew most of the time, but because of the unpredictable weather in February and March, he drove in those months. The difference was an hour and a half to drive it and .rm 7.00"

15 minutes to fly!"

At first, Deter flew the triangle every other day, but with Doc Bar's growing fame, the breeding business became an every-day chore. In the beginning of Doc Bar's breeding career, artificial insemination was not yet popular, so Doc Bar live-covered his mares. Thankfully, he wasn't a picky stallion. As long as the mare was hobbled and her tail wrapped, the stallion proved to be very dependable. If a mare wouldn't hobble, she would not be bred, eliminating the possibility of injury to the stallion.

"Doc was a machine," remembered Charlie. "He was so easy to breed; I'd come up here to this barn and get him, lead him down to the other barn, where we'd have a mare ready, and it took us not over five minutes. He just wasn't any trouble. I could hold him and wash him, then lead him up to the mare and he didn't wait or stand around; he got the job done. Our vet had a lot of affection for him and nicknamed him Docky."

Later, in his breeding career, artificial insemination made breeding easier and increased the number of mares he got in foal.

"He was just an incredible stallion," said Dr. Deter. "Some stallions get cranky in a breeding program but Doc Bar was just a good citizen. He faithfully did his job every day."

With Doc Bar's fame, owners with famous mares wanted a colt sired by Doc Bar. The process, however, was not always an easy one because age added so many additional factors to the breeding process.

"We had so many mares to breed!" recalled Deter, a task that on some days seemed almost overwhelming. "Of course, owners with particularly famous, but old mares, wanted a foal by Doc Bar, and those would be difficult since you were breeding an older stallion to an older mare. Now, if you'd always had a band of nice virgin mares, that would have been easy!"

Deter utilized the nearby Davis University's facilities when breeding Doc Bar. "I flew Dr. John Hughes and Dr. Kent Fowler to the ranch for them to check Doc Bar for me from time to time, to see if there was something we should be doing different. I didn't want to take a chance on missing out on anything with him. I felt like we shouldn't leave any stones unturned, he was just such a special horse."

Stephenie acknowledged that the stallion was easy to handle, but still he was a stallion. Once in a while, he needed to try Charlie, just to make sure who was the boss.

"You could see it building," laughed Stephenie. "He'd push Charlie so far, then Charlie had to rattle his chain. He was so smart, he knew when he had overstepped his boundaries. He'd make a big scream and then jump way back, as if to say, 'okay, you're still boss.' "

Approximately 50 mares, in addition to their own broodmares, were on the Doc Bar Ranch at one time and responsibility surpassed just getting them bred. Many owners sent pregnant mares to the ranch to foal out, so the mares could be bred back immediately on foal heat. Sleepless nights spent foaling mares and long days spent breeding them ran endlessly together. Doc Bar, himself, however, required little attention.

Throughout Doc Bar's breeding career, there were few problems on the ranch. One sunny afternoon, however, Mother Nature demanded her share of the attention.

"One of the last years that we bred Doc, Charlie's dad and I were getting a mare ready to breed. He was holding her and I was bent, about to hobble her. Charlie had already come in with Doc Bar and was waiting on me.

"All of a sudden, we had this enormous earthquake. With that first tremor, fear ran through me and without a moment's hesitation, I jumped up from there and ran from the barn, Charlie's Dad right behind me. Of course, that left Charlie in the barn holding the stud with a loose mare who was in heat right beside them.

"We could hear him screaming over the rumble to come back, but neither one of us paid any attention to him," laughed Stephenie.

Clouds of heavy dust began a slow ascent from the quaking ground while rocks and boulders of all size tumbled from the surrounding mountains. The quake ended as quickly as it started, leaving buildings and people, although shaken, none the worse for nature's shudder.

When the excitement subsided, Mr. Ward and Stephenie cautiously returned to the breeding barn, hearing frightful silence rather than expected commotion. There, in the middle of the barn, stood a stunned Charlie Ward. Doc Bar, whose lead rope lay relaxed in Charlie's hand, waited patiently, undisturbed by the disorder or the loose mare standing close by.

## The End of Fertility

In 1975, 41 foals were sired by the stallion, while 42 foals were born in 1976. By then, Doc Bar, a 1956 foal, had reached the age of 20. The years began dropping subtle signs that his breeding career was approaching its end.

"We were keeping tabs on the number of live motile cells that he produced, because that dictates how many mares you can inseminate on a daily basis," explained Dr. Deter. "We were collecting him daily and trying to distribute collection as well as we could. Although we were looking at numbers that were below normal, mares were still conceiving, so who argues with that."

But in 1977, the breeding career of the most famous cutting horse stallion in the industry came to an abrupt end.

"When it went, it went," sighed Deter.

By then, the Doc Bar Ranch had stopped receiving outside mares. One mare belonging to the Jensens conceived in 1978. Appropriately, they named him Doc's Last Chance.

# 13

## The Progeny

*What does the future hold? Much of the past has a way of repeating itself. We handled the past and we can do even better in the future, for hindsight can give us a little foresight, not specifically but generally.*

*The best thing about the future is that it comes upon us by degrees, a day at a time. We can manage that much.*

"Today is Mine" by Larry Brownlow,
Brownlow Publishing Company, Inc., 1972

\*\*\*

That for which he was most famous, Doc Bar never did. While today's colts have to prove themselves, Doc Bar's proof was in his heritage, not in his performance. Although he is best known as the sire of cutting champions, since his offspring dominated the event, his get also achieved prominence in almost every performance area. A few examples were Barlet and Doc's Tami Bar in halter, Fizzabar and Janie Bar in hackamore and Doc's Dee Bar, the all-around horse. Where there was a need for intelligence and athletic ability, he imparted it.

## The Futurities:

The birth of the National Cutting Horse Association Futurity in 1962, a proving ground for 3-year-old horses, quickly became the most prestigious cutting event to win. The year the event was born, Doc Bar, a pretty halter horse who had never entered a cutting arena, but whose get were destined to dominate Futurity championships, was purchased by Dr. and Mrs. Jensen.

Seven years later, in 1969, when Doc Bar was 13 years old, his offspring gained attention at the NCHA Futurity. Following that year, his get continually gained momentum and year after year they gave command performances in the Will Rogers Arena at Fort Worth, Texas.

## 1969

His lineage in the cutting horse industry first sparkled for attention at the 1969 NCHA Futurity when Doc Bar offspring lined up for second-, third- and fourth-place wins. Doc's Kitty was the NCHA Futurity Reserve Champion, Doc Luck Bar earned third-place honors and Doc's Leo Lad captured fourth place. In addition, Doc's Blue Bar was also a finalist.

"From that year on, people wanted to ride them," stated Charlie Ward. "When I would leave here going to the Futurity, I would look like a Gypsy horse trader! I'd have my own futurity horse plus three or more 2-year-olds to sell. I'd stop in Arizona along the way and sell one or two, then people in Fort Worth at the Futurity would get upset with me because I'd sold 'em!"

## 1970

When Doc Bar's son, Doc O' Lena, swept all four go-rounds of the Futurity the following year, "Doc Bar mania" exploded. Doc O' Lena, however, wasn't the only Doc Bar horse to excel in the 1970 Futurity. Doc's Carolyn placed third while Doc's Date Bar tied for fourth, Doc's Blue Lou was a finalist and Doc's Music Man was a semifinalist.

## 1971

In 1971, when Doc O' Lena's full brother, Dry Doc, won the coveted Futurity title, the victory poured fuel to an already raging Doc Bar delirium. Eleven Doc Bar sons and daughters had entered the prestigious cutting and in addition to Dry Doc's win, Doc's Snow Flake split second through fifth while Doc Holiday, Doc's Blue Frost, Doc's Jack Frost, Doc's Ginger Bar and Doc's Twister made the semifinals.

## 1972

Returning in 1972, Doc's Tlell, earned fourth place in the Futurity. Two other Doc Bar offspring, Doc's Lynx, and Doc's

Nanaimo, get tied for fifth, sixth and seventh places while Doc's Haida tied for top honors in the semifinals. The Doc Bar lineage continued to roll.

## 1973

Once again, in 1973, a Doc Bar get, Doc's Marmoset, won the Futurity thus re-establishing the trend of Doc Bar descendants seizing the "gold" NCHA crown. In addition, Nu Bar tied for first and second in the semifinals, while Doc's Leopard earned eighth place. Other Doc Bar get to make the limelight that year were Doc Tari, Doc's Bar Tab, Doc's Coyote, Doc's Dulce Bar, Doc's Sug, Doc's Topi and The Red Baron.

The first of Doc Bar grand-get, Dee Bars Beaver by Doc's Dee Bar, out of Revlon Beaver by Red Beaver, was also a finalist.

Just a few years earlier, in 1969, the NCHA Non-Professional Futurity had been introduced and before long Doc Bar get were shining there also. Doc Quixote won the 1973 Non-Professional Futurity while another Doc Bar son, Doc Tari, was Reserve Champion. The Red Baron, Doc's Dulce Bar and Moon Doc were finalists.

According to "The Doc Bar Heritage," written by Cathy Dixon for the Quarter Horse Journal, "Doc Bar had 18 sons and daughters entered in the Futurity with 10 in the semifinals and three in the finals. Five of his get placed in the Non-Pro." (June, 1979, p. 85)

## 1974

By the time another offspring, Doc's Yuba Lea, won the 1974 Futurity and Doc's Bar Gal, Doc's Tulare and Doc's Ventura finished as finalists, Doc Bar get had solidly established their sire as "King" of the cutting horse sires. Leantoo, a Doc O' Lena progeny and a Doc Bar grand-get, won the 1974 Non-Professional Futurity.

## 1975

Another first at the NCHA Futurity happened when Lenaette, by Futurity winner Doc O' Lena by Doc Bar, won the championship. Besides being the first foal of a futurity winner to win the futurity, from the seven years since Doc Bar get made their march on the Futurity championships (1969 entries), a Doc Bar get or grand-get had won five titles while another get had won a reserve title. Leantoo's 1974 Non-Professional Futurity title and Lenaette's 1975 Open Futurity title ratified Doc Bar's cutting potency.

That year also, Doc's Willi Winki finished third while Boon Bar and Doc's Lady Madonna were finalists. Grand-get sired by Doc O'Lena fared well in the Non-Professional Division with three placing in the top ten.

## 1976

Although a Doc Bar progeny did not win the Futurity, plenty of offspring racked up honors for the stallion. Doc's Becky by Docs Lynx by Doc Bar continued the tradition by winning Reserve Champion. Doc's Remedy and Doc's Oak split fourth through sixth place while Doc's Steady Date took seventh place. Doc Bar Tonette, Doc Wilson, Doc's Hickory, Doc's Madron and Doc's Mahogany were finalists. Doc Sox, by Doc Tari by Doc Bar, won the Non-Professional Co-Championship.

## 1977

Once again, a Doc Bar get took home the Reserve Championship title when Doc's Serendipity captured the 1977 Futurity Reserve Championship title. Three Doc Bar get, Doc's Little Bit, Doc O'Lock and Doc's Wrangler split fifth through eighth place. Docs Marsala and Doc's Flying Bar were also finalists.

That year, two Doc Bar-bred horses shared co-championships in the Non-Pro. Chickasha Ann Doc by Doc Quixote by Doc Bar and Bar O'Lena by Doc O'Lena. By the late seventies, Doc Bar get and grand-get, multiplying like sands of the sea, were running away with titles in cuttings across the country.

## 1978

Again a grand-get of Doc Bar, Lynx Melody, by Doc's Lynx, won the Futurity while the Reserve Champion went to Docs Poco Doc by Boon Bar. Docs Tin Lizzie finished third while Docs Star Chex and Docs Taxi Dancer split fifth through eighth place. Holey Doc Sox split 14th and 15th. In the semifinals, Docs Linda split fourth and fifth and Docs Peppy Belle was a finalist.

"Five of the finishers were by Doc Bar and five by his offspring. The Non-Pro Division was equally dominated by the Doc Bar line. Of the 122 originally entered, 16 made it to the Finals..." (Doc Bar Heritage, June, 1979, p.86)

## 1979

Gay Doc split sixth and seventh place in the Futurity while Doc O Chex, Doc Bars Best, Docatres, Docs Brown Sugar, Docs Budha, Docs Rey Jey, Doc's Sweet Glow and Docs Voyager were finalist. Docs Diablo, by Doc's Prescription by Doc Bar, was the Co-Reserve Futurity Champion in 1979.

## 1980

Doc Bar was no longer breeding. The last year that Doc Bar get entered the Futurity, Doc Jensen split eighth through 11th place, Doctor Montoya and Genuine Doc were finalists. His legacy, although protected by his grand-get, would now be totally left in the hands of his progeny.

The progeny continued to do well in the eighties. Probably the most famous of all his grand-get is Smart Little Lena, which, with total earnings of $577,652.36, won the "Triple Crown of Cutting," - the NCHA Futurity, Super Stakes and Derby. In 1983, Docs Okie Quixote, another grand-get, became a second Triple Crown winner. In 1984, Doc Per, a great grand-get, won two legs of the coveted triple crown.

In 1985, The Gemnist, by Doc Bar Gem, a son of Doc Bar, won the prestigious NCHA Futurity; in 1987, Smart Date, a double-bred Doc Bar, won the event; 1988 saw Smart Little Senor, another son of Smart Little Lena in the winner's circle, and in 1989 the winner's check went to July Jazz, a grandson of Doc Quixote.

To date, the 1990s have been a clean sweep for Doc Bar-bred Futurity Champions: Millie Montana, sired by Montana Doc by Doc O'Lena, came in first in 1990; 1991 saw Little Tenina, out of Tenino Fair by Doc Bar, win; in 1992 it was Dox Miss N Reno, out of Paloma Quixote by Doc Quixote, crowned the champion; in 1993, it was Bobs Smokin Joe, sired by Bob Acre Doc by Son Ofa Doc by Doc Bar, in the winner's circle and in 1994, CD Olena, a son of Doc O'Lena, took the title.

## NCHA Hall Of Fame:

While Fizzabar was the first Doc Bar get to enter the NCHA Hall of Fame, Doc's Starlight, who also won the 1978 NCHA World Championship Finals, also entered the Hall of Fame, a feat not easily accomplished. According to the qualifications established by the NCHA Executive Board, the mission of the NCHA Hall of Fame was to honor horses who proved their excellence at the grass roots level of cutting, which were not the high-dollar aged events, but rather the weekend NCHA-approved shows.

"To give the cutting horse greater recognition, an NCHA Hall of Fame has been established to credit famous cutting horses. To be placed in the Hall of Fame, a horse must win $35,000* in NCHA Open Championship Contests. Upon winning the $35,000* a Gold Certificate will be issued to the owner of the horse and a plaque with the horse's and owner's name will be placed on the walls of the NCHA office. Recipients of the NCHA Hall of Fame Award have also received a Platinum, Gold, Silver and Bronze Award.

Although many Doc Bar get competed only in aged events and won enough money to qualify them for the Hall of Fame, since they did not win the dollars in NCHA Open Championship contests, they were ineligible for Hall of Fame status. In addition to Fizzabar and Doc's Starlight, Dry Doc, Doc's Oak, Doc's Playmate and Doc Wilson entered the distinguished NCHA Hall of Fame.

## Other Events:

While numerous Doc Bar get were taken to competitions other than cutting, perhaps Doc's Dee Bar, a 1963 foal out of Lura Tivio received the most attention for his all-around abilities and numerous championships.

"I bought Doc's Dee Bar when he was 10 months old from Charley Araujo for a group of builders who had formed a corporation," stated trainer Don Avila of Oregon. "In fact, they started a stable and named it Bar Nothing Farms. I showed Doc's Dee Bar until he was a 2-year-old for them at which time they had a little financial slump so I bought him."

*1980, amended to $50,000; 1981, amended to $100,000; 1985, amended to $150,000; 1989, amended to $200,000; 1991, amended to $150,000 (National Cutting Horses Association NCHA Yearbook).

Avila's faith in the stallion to continue to do well in the competitive world prompted him to make the purchase. Not only had he shown Doc's Dee Bar and done well, but Charley Araujo, had also shown him as a yearling with great success.

"I thought he was one of the best things going at the time. I believe he was the only yearling ever to go Grand Champion in an "A" show which he did with Charley Araujo."

Avila, rather than retain the stallion only in halter classes, branched out into numerous performance events, showing him in nine different classes.

"He was a really good horse," stressed Avila. "I'd take him to shows where he would win anywhere from three to six of the classes and place in all of the others. Of course, a horse working in eight or nine events is not going to be as good as one that is a specialized horse in one field, but he was a great western riding horse, hard to beat in western pleasure and a terrific heeling and calf horse. He wanted to be a good reining horse if a guy had just taken him and done it.

In "The Doc Bar Influence in Cutting" published in The Quarter Horse Journal, Anna Robertson stated, "Doc's Dee Bar has proven himself in the AQHA show arena, having earned 273 performance points in eight event and 170 halter points with 63 grands and 28 reserves. He has been the Oregon high-point stallion on numerous occasions, and has over 40 all-around titles." (Jan. 1973, p. 122)

Avila, who stated that Doc's Dee Bar was an easy horse to train, remembers four specials shows to which he took the great stallion over a two-year spread: Walla Walla, Washington; Santa Rosa, California; Roseburg, Oregon and Grants Pass, Oregon. At each show Avila entered Doc's Dee Bar in nine events and won all nine of them.

"He was just a really a good horse," stressed Avila. "I guess my big limelight with Doc's Dee Bar was when I won 18 All-Around saddles on him in one year. When he died, although Janie Bar had the most halter points of Doc Bar colts, he had more halter and performance points than any son of Doc Bar."

## Doc Bar: For The Record

When Doc Bar retired from service in 1978, he had sired 485 registered foals. According to 1995 AQHA records, he had sired 101 open halter-point earners who had earned 2,492 points and 13 youth halter-point earners, who had earned 250.5 points.

The 207 performance-horse earners have accumulated 4,576.5 points, while six Amateur performance-point earners have earned 59.5 points. Twenty-four youth performance-point earners have earned 15,015 points.

In addition, 118 Doc Bar performance get have received Register Of Merit certificates while one Amateur and 15 youth have received ROM certificates.

Doc Bar progeny have won two AQHA World Championships, four Reserve World Championships and include 27 AQHA Open Champions. From his progeny, 18 open horses have won 20 Superior honors with the American Quarter Horse Association.

According to statistics compiled by **Equi-Stat,** a division of Quarter Horse News, a semi-monthly publication, in cutting-horse competition, Doc Bar led both the paternal grandsires in 1993, with $938,937, and the maternal grandsires with $468,195. The next year, in 1994, he again led the paternal grandsires with $1,151,181 and the maternal grandsires with $428,851. In 1995, while he still led the paternal grandsires with $893,869, on the maternal grandsires chart, he sat third with $310,947.

## The Future:

"Times change and you change with them, we didn't pay attention to pedigrees years ago, but then King Fritz and Doc Bar came along. You couldn't ignore their babies, they were winners," said Bobby Ingersoll in Theresa Fox's article titled "Bob Ingersoll" in the February 10, 1995, issue of Quarter Horse News.

As the horse world realized that the get of Doc Bar were winners, they beat a path to his door with their mares, producing outstanding get, which then were bred to other outstanding Doc Bar get, which were again bred to other outstanding Doc Bar get. From years of continual inbreeding, Doc Bar blood now saturates some pedigrees, too much so for the family who stood him to greatness.

"Today, there is a need for more substance, more stifle,

more strength back there," reflected Charlie Ward. "We've bred Doc Bar blood to Doc Bar blood so much that we're losing some of that. When you start losing muscle then the rest of the program is going to get a little weak."

Stephenie Ward agrees with her husband. The couple, who today stand Grays Starlight, a stallion with Doc Bar- Poco Tivio blood, strongly advocate crossing him only on mares that do not have the same dominant genes.

"I'm really concerned about how they keep in-breeding," stated Stephenie. "I'm concerned about the fertility and the soundness of the offspring. I think we have already seen problems and if we continue breeding the way we are, we may get horses that can't stand up."

Inbreeding is usually done to create a genetically better horse since a foal that is inbred will have more of the genetic make-up of desired ancestors. Most lineage studies of successful horses have common ancestors within eight generations in their pedigrees and such inbreeding can be an enhancement to outstanding breeding programs.

It is too much of a good thing, however, that causes the problem. When the process continues generation after generation, the benefits peak and then backfire, causing problem to start rising. According to the college text, "Modern Genetics," written by Franco J. Ayala and John A. Kiger, "Breeders have long known that inbreeding usually leads to a reduction in fitness, owing to deterioration in important attributes, such as fertility, vigor, and resistance to disease."

Jay Pumphrey, a long-time advocate of the study of genetics and past president of the American Quarter Horse Association, agrees that too much of the same blood can cause problems. "Any time you concentrate too much of the same blood with any livestock, you're liable to have a latent genetic factor crop out. For example, we got dwarfism in cattle from a double recessive gene. It hit the Hereford business in the 40s real strong and it took until 1954 to learn where it came from."

"In horses, " continued Pumphrey, if you inbreed too much, you shorten the pastern on them, and end up with a rough ride. Or, if you continually breed small hoof to small hoof, before long, they're not going to have anyting to stand on and you're going to get into trouble."

Larry Thornton, a pedigree analyst and regular contributor to the Southern Horseman magazine, stated, " The idea in line breeding is to get his good traits by increasing the blood percentage of Doc Bar. If we continue to use it again and again though, we lose variation. When you lose genetic variation in our breeding program then you cease to breed improvement."

That is the genetic predicament that the Wards fear unless Doc Bar blood is balanced by the blood of different pedigrees. As trainer Ingersoll stated, "Times change ... The Wards, who stood Doc Bar to greatness, believe it's time to change with them."

# 14

## Myth Versus Reality

*Myth: A traditional story of unknown authorship, ostensibly with a historical basis, but serving usually to explain some phenonomen of nature ... a fictitious story or some unscientific account.*

*Reality: the quality of being real; a person or thing that is real; fact.*

*** 

For years, it was an unintentionally kept secret that Doc Bar had a full brother which had also been sold at an early age. Even the Finleys had forgotten about the stallion until Doc Bar's fame surfaced. Curiously, Tom Finley checked with the American Quarter Horse Association in Amarillo to see who owned the horse at that time.

"We had sold him to a fella in New Mexico; he still had him and hadn't done anything with him. About that same time though, quite a few trainers heard about him and tried to buy the horse, but they couldn't get it done. Dandy Doll had some other foals by our own horses but we never bred her out anymore after those two colts were born."

### Doc Bar: Quarter Horse Genes

It is, therefore, unknown if Doc Bar's full brother could have sired outstanding performances horses like Doc Bar did. The fact that many horsemen tried to buy the stallion, though, says they thought so and felt his purchase would be a worthwhile gamble.

The answer is all in the genetics, that mysterious phenomena that makes some horses bay and some sorrel and what sometimes resembles a bag of jumbled sticks. What seems like it should be, is often just the opposite; what seems like it shouldn't favor, often is just alike. For example, trainer Jack Brainard, who rode Doc Bar, remembered the horse to be insensitive to minor leg-and-foot movement.

"It's the strangest thing, the laws of genetics, I suppose," suggested Brainard. "Most of Doc Bar's colts are 'feely feely' horses; in fact, some are almost too sensitive to touch. That's directly opposite of their sire."

Sometimes there seems to be no rhyme or reason to genetics and trainer Don Dodge calls that "the nick." "It's just when, for whatever reason, the pairing of the genes is outstanding. That's what they call a good nick. The only times in my life that I saw it work, was Doc Bar's colts and the colts of Poco Tivio and Sheilwin - Poco Sandra, Poco Champ, Poco Lena. Sheilwin, by the way, was never ridden."

While Dodge referred to the crossing of the genes as a nick, Jay Pumphrey, former general manager of the Burnett Estates and past president of AQHA, referred to the offspring of such a "nick" as a stopper. In an article, "Where Do We Go From Here," by Sally Harrison for her book, The Cutting Horse, Pumphrey gave a theory about these genetic mysteries.

"From observing horses and cattle, I have discovered some animals that I call stoppers. Two different lines come together and hit with the right combinations of genes that seem to defy the odds. Maybe that's what makes these animals great performers. All the good genes for certain qualities have come together in a combination that make them superior performers and /or breeders. Everything in the pedigree is stopped behind them and that individual starts things from there on and begins a superior influence on his offspring. You might say that the special genetic blend of superior genes stops the varied makeup of the previous ancestors." (Feb 1992, p. 18.)

Whatever the reason, the genetics of Lightning Bar crossed with Dandy Doll produced a foal that revolutionized the cutting industry. In fact, the foal was such a contrast to other foals of that time that some horse people questioned his breeding.

Poco Tivio in his later years.

## The Arabian Rumor:

There was a time when rumor ran rampant that Doc Bar was part Arabian. His smaller size and his unique head only attributed to the rumor. Don Hemstrom, the young cowboy on the Finley ranch who carried Dandy Doll to Lightning Bar for breeding, found the rumor amusing because he knew better, but understood how such a thing got started.

"He was such a cute, tiny horse, with a tiny head. He stood out like a sore thumb among the rest of those colts. That's why he attracted so much attention."

Artist Keith Christie, who sculpted a bronze of Doc Bar for the Pacific Coast Quarter Horse Association, gave his own explanation why many thought Doc Bar had Arabian characteristics.

"When I went to photograph Doc Bar for the bronze, what surprised me was his head," said Christie. "I'd always heard about his Arab look and the dish in his face. There was no dish face. His nose was as straight as a ruler. He did have an offset blaze though, and that gave him a dish-face impression."

Trainer Jack Brainard, also debunking the myth, recalled personal experience to methodically explain why Doc Bar veins did not carry Arabian blood.

"I don't think there is an ounce of Arab in Doc Bar. You couldn't put any Arab in that horse at all and have him as quiet and dead-bellied as he was. I don't care if he is only a 1/4 Arab, these things show up quick. Besides, he didn't ride like any part Arab and I've ridden lots of Arabs."

Past AQHA President, Lee Berwick, who avows that Three Bars made the greatest contribution to the Quarter Horse breed, believes it was Three Bars, the grandsire of Doc Bar, which contributed to Doc Bar's refinement and good head, the physical attributes to which doubters pointed when advocating Doc Bar was not a Quarter Horse.

Aside from the words of the employee who carried the mare to be bred to Lightning Bar, aside from a trainer's point of view, aside from the artist who sculpted him, the Finley family, owners of Dandy Doll, stated Lightning Bar to be the sire and that should be enough.

According to pedigree analyst Larry Thornton, "The Finley family had an outstanding reputation in the horse industry and, therefore, had too much at stake to falsify registration papers.

"This reminds me of an interview I had with Lowell Hankins," continued Thornton, "on the possibility of Standardbred blood in the pedigree of King. He (Lowell) said, 'I don't know...somebody wrote an article one time that King wasn't bred the way they said he was. Jess was worried that King wasn't like he was supposed to be bred. It worried Jess, I said to Jess, 'Buddy, that horse is an old horse and he is proven... I'm sure he was bred like Benevides said he was. They didn't have that kind of reputation. Horses were a nickel a dozen in those days and times. There was no need of changing it. It wouldn't benefit them to change it.' "

The moral of Thornton's story fits the Finleys. Just as there was no benefit to gain by Benevides falsifying the breeding of King, there was no benefit to be gained by the Finleys falsifying the breeding of Doc Bar.

## The Arabian Facts:

Even though highly qualified equine people attest to the Quarter Horse breeding of Doc Bar, the statement still surfaces periodically that, "He sure looks like he has some Arab in him." Probably, he does.

No more so, however, than the majority of the horses being ridden today. The fact is summed up in one statement in the Family Table of Race Horses, a 1990 publication written by Toru Shira. Stated Shira, ""All horses have Arabian background in them. " And then he drew the ancestral map to prove it.

"Genetics is all a map," explained Pumphrey, "and if you learn to read it, you'll learn an awful lot. "

Doc Bar's sire, Lightning Bar, being a son of a Thoroughbred, carried Doc Bar one step closer to his original ancestors with their Arabian blood.

"The Thoroughbred is the fastest and most valuable of the world's breeds, and around it has grown a huge racing and breeding industry. It evolved in England in the 17th and 18th centuries as a result of the crossing of imported Arabian stallions with a native stock of "running horses." (The Ultimate Horse Book: Edwyn Hartley Edwards. Dorling Kindersley, Inc. New York. p34.)

"Many people don't realize that most Quarter Horses and theoretically all Thoroughbreds trace to the foundation sires Byerley Turk, the Darley Arabian and the Godolphin Arabian. So the "breeds" or types of horses we call the Arabian, the Turk or the Barb are the foundation of most of our modern breeds," stated Thornton.

"Doc Bar's sire line traces to the Darley Arabian," he continued. "Porte Drapeau is the sire of My Texas Dandy, the grandsire of Dandy Doll, the dam of Doc Bar. Porte Drapeau traces his sire line to the Darley Arabian.

"As breeders planning a mating, we are trying to put a genetic code together in the individual being produced. This is especially true when we linebreed back to a great horse. We are trying to duplicate the genetic code that made that horse so important. Sometimes, through natural selection, we can see traits that have been lost for generations come back to the surface and express themselves. Who is to say this is not what happened to Doc Bar?" suggested Thornton.

## Speculation:

Besides these cold, hard statistics, there is also speculation, and conjecture which, if not more colorful, is usually more fun to consider than fact. For example, what if a mare in the Doc Bar lineage got "exposed" unknowingly?

"Years back somebody might have had an Arabian that jumped the fence and bred a mare," suggested Pumphrey when pressured to play the game. "There's a possibility that Streak's mother by Lone Star got exposed, and that blood came into Texas Dandy.

"Of Course, Lightning Bar was a mutton-withered little fella, a great breeding horse but pretty tight withered. I don't know where that came from in him. So who knows, he could be the culprit with Arabian Blood, " stated Pumphrey, ending his guessing game.

One to consider when playing with speculation, is Della P, the dam of Lightning Bar, which possessed a rather illustrious background. Larry Thornton in his article "Reading a Pedigree," for Southern Horseman magazine, stated," The Stud Book tells us that Della P was sired by Doc Horn. Art Pollard, the last owner of Della P, readily confessed that he really didn't know if Doc Horn was actually her sire. They just went by what they were told when Dink Parker purchased the mare out of Louisiana.

"Lloyd Gary, a student of the cajun bred running horse, tells us that Louisiana Henry or The Dun Horse, a he was called by some, was the sire of Della P. Gary bases his belief on information he gathered from horsemen like Claud Morien (the breeder of Light Foot Sis, the mother of Go Man Go). Gary credits this error to the fact that Della P did have a half sister that was sired by Doc Horn."

Such a suggestion was not so rare years ago when pedigrees were taken less seriously. Proof of the lax pedigree information lies with the dam of Oklahoma Star which has three different pedigrees. Clean blood lines will only register after we pass those generations of unknown horses in a pedigree and with the desire to keep better records. Even then though, there will be the possibility that someone jumped the fence one night.

## Cow Sense:

Bob Denhart, in his article "The Story Behind Doc Bar," for the _Western Horseman_ magazine, claims Sidney Vail, an owner of Three Bars, gave his stallion the credit for the cow sense ability passed to Doc Bar offspring.

"One day Sidney and I were discussing Doc Bar's great ability to produce cutting horses. He said that he had kept Three Bars in a corral with his roping calves and that when the horse did not have anything else to do, he would cut out a calf and dodge him around. He added that he brought home all of Three Bars' colts that couldn't win at the track and started roping on them. He said they all had enough sense to follow a cow."

It all returns to genetics. The importance is not so much the historical proof of where the genes originated as is the evidence of what the genes are. For Doc Bar, it is his get, rather than his ancestral blood, that solidifies him as a champion performance breeder with pretty good looks to go with it.

# 15

## The Golden Years

*Grow old along with me
The best is yet to be -
The last of life for which the first was made,*
                    *Browning*

***

Amateur photographer, non-pro cutter and college professor, Bill Baldwin, knew what he wanted to do. For years, he had worked diligently to upgrade the agricultural program for Riverside City College and now he felt it was time to visit other schools, to view their programs and retrieve new ideas. He knew he wanted to take a sabbatical and travel the state of California.

Taking a leave from the clock-punching regularity of tedious classroom activities would also grant him the freedom to live a dream. Baldwin had become a good acquaintance with the Wards, the caretakers of the famous horse, Doc Bar, and as a part-time photographer, he dreamed of one day photographing the horse standing among the swaying grasses of his domain, surrounded by the beautiful hills of Paicines, the perfect setting and backdrop.

As soon as the college "powers that be" granted the sabbatical leave, Baldwin called the Wards. It was the right time of year and the relief from pressing school obligations freed his mind to capture creativity. He wanted to photograph the great Doc Bar.

## Photos for Posterity

The day of his appointment with the Wards and their horse dawned crystal clear. While Baldwin traveled the gravel road just before reaching the Doc Bar Ranch, clouds of dust billowing behind his car, he glanced for probably the hundredth time out of the car window, craning his head for a better view of the sky. It promised him a great day for photography.

Stephenie and Charlie greeted their friend with the famous hospitality for which they were noted. After the normal amenities and a few moments of casual conversation, Charlie, observant to the ways of visitors anxiously waiting to see the ranch celebrity, quickly detected Baldwin's shifting weight and searching eyes.

Smiling, Charlie pointed him toward the barn where, after grabbing a halter, the two men headed for a nearby pasture. There, Charlie merely strolled out to Doc Bar, whose head was down grazing in the field. The stallion, without moving, slowly raised his head and looked toward Charlie, his way of greeting an old friend. Charlie, rather than put the halter on the horse, casually latched it around Doc Bar's neck, gave him an affectionate pat and then led him back toward Baldwin.

"Charlie brought Doc Bar to the middle of a big alfalfa field, where I stood with my back to a big pen of mares, and the minute he saw my camera, he walked right into a pose," laughed Bill, remembering the stallion's personality. "It was as if he knew what I was there for and he immediately puffed up and struck that famous pose. I was impressed! Of course, he also saw his mares behind me and thought he was in "seventh heaven."

Baldwin had good reason to be impressed. He had wrestled with many stallions in photography sessions, struggling to get them in the correct position and then to snap the right expression. Photographing animals was not an easy profession.

"So often, you have to out-think these horses to get them to set up for you," stated Baldwin, who has since left teaching behind for full-time photography. If he is a show horse, which has had his picture taken a million times, posing for another one may be the last thing he wants to do, so getting cooperation isn't always easy. A lot of times a horse won't brighten up for you, or if he does, it's only for a short time."

That, however, wasn't the case with Doc Bar which, although he had posed for hundreds of pictures, liked the limelight. "He was a very funny horse," laughed Stephenie. "There was a big mound in the pen where he stayed and so many times when people came to see him, they wanted to take pictures. As soon as they pointed a camera at him, he'd go on that mound, straighten his legs and pose. He always did have a lot of personality."

## Out to Pasture

For Doc Bar, it was the best of times. Since he was unable to breed mares, he had been released to the wide-open spaces of a large pasture across the river. No longer did confinement in a stall and a run possess him, since he was finally turned out to roam at his free will. Occasionally, he kicked up his heels and ran around the field, acting more like a young colt than an old stallion. Mostly, however, Doc Bar grazed the green grass and enjoyed the companionship of mares.

"That was when he was happiest," remembered Stephenie. "We had a big pasture across the river with a lot of old mares and colts in it and we turned him out with them. He loved it."

Although Doc Bar no longer lived only yards from their home, Stephenie or Charlie, or sometimes both of them, daily checked on the stallion. At that time, in his twenties, Doc Bar was considered an old horse with only a limited number of years left and the two felt a strong duty to monitor his health closely. Doc Bar, however, roamed the pastures with his mares for almost another 15 years, longer than he stood at stud, before age and its infirmities took its toll.

Slowly, with the passing years, Charlie brought Doc Bar, little by little, pasture by pasture, back to the central ranch until once again he stood, as he had for years, within yards of their home. Charlie wanted the stallion, which now ran no more, close to him, just in case he needed immediate attention.

At first, Doc Bar moved to the home side of the river; then into a larger pasture, closer to the barns; then just across the road from the house and finally to a small trap nearby. Always, though, with each move, Doc Bar took his companion mares with him.

## Frieda Visits Doc Bar

Time and again, Doc Bar outlived his companion mares and one day, when the stallion was 33 years old, Stephenie lamented to her friend, Sue Hearst, how once again they were searching for a companion for Doc Bar.

"I happened to have just the girl!" exclaimed Sue. "Frieda's 29 years old, although she doesn't look it, and she's a neat, old mare."

Stephenie, relieved that Doc Bar would once again have a friend, was delighted that the Hearsts, who lived only an hour away, could bring the mare right over.

George and Sue Hearst pulled slowly down the Ward's long driveway and unloaded Frieda. Doc Bar, standing in a pasture at the beginning of the entrance, watched intently, ears erect and body rigid, as Sue led Frieda back up the driveway toward his pasture. The closer she came with the mare, the more the stallion, anticipating a new friend, blustered with excitement.

"He was strutting, nickering, talking and prancing up and down the fence," laughed Sue. "He was really excited to see her and it was so fun to watch him."

After she let Frieda loose in the pasture, the two horses, as if age was no longer a factor, flirted continuously with one another. They nickered, grunted and nuzzled one another with heads raised, vying for one another's attention. It looked as if the two would make a great pair for the rest of their lives.

Yet, it didn't happen that way. As months passed, Charlie noticed the outline of Doc Bar's ribs against his skin. Curiously, he examined the stallion. Doc Bar didn't act like he felt bad, but since he had always been an easy keeper, his growing thin made no sense. So for several days, Charlie, purposely watched the stallion and his new girlfriend from a distance at feeding time. It didn't take long to realize the problem.

"It was so embarrassing," laughed Sue. "We had to go get our mare and bring her home because she wasn't letting Doc Bar have anything to eat! They fed pellets to Doc Bar and she loved them!

Once again, the Hearsts made the trip to Paicines, but this time to pick up Frieda, slick and fat from her days of dominating Doc Bar at the feed trough.

Eventually, however, the deterioration of Doc Bar's teeth, forced the Wards to place him in a special trap. Although he lived and ate by himself, thus removing competition for his alfalfa pellets and molasses, a pasture of mares beside him kept him company.

# 16

## *The Cow Palace*

*For Yesterday is only a Dream
And To-Morrow is only a Vision
But To-Day well lived,
Makes every yesterday
A dream of Happiness,
And every To-Morrow a Vision of Hope*

>*Leaves of Gold.
The Coslett Publishing Company,
Williamsport, Pa., p.171*

\*\*\*

The Grand National Horse Show, a combination horse show, stock show and rodeo held yearly at the Cow Palace, paralleled the play-offs for the National Finals Rodeo since it was the last show of the year to qualify for any Finals events. The Pacific Coast Quarter Horse Association, the host of the Quarter Horse Show of the Grand National, added spice to their event by returning past champions. The presentation ceremonies grew to be one of the most important activities of the show and all other events stopped for the presentation. The year, 1981, had an extraordinary program just for Doc Bar.

### A Special Award:

"Don Pabst, who is now deceased, had the idea of bringing back the Cow Palace champions that were still living," remembered Roger McMahan, a Pacific Coast Quarter Horse

Association Director at that time. "It had been a successful part of the Grand National for several years but that particular year, since Doc Bar was so famous, we decided to specially honor him."

The association requested that artist Keith Christie do a sculpture of Doc Bar to be presented to the Jensens during the ceremony. Christie, who did Western paints, but neither portraits nor sculptures, was concerned whether the project would be a profitable one. He expressed that concern to Duane Pettibone, a PCQHA director, as the two of them worked out the details of the sculpture. To compensate Christie for the cost, Pettibone suggested that a special edition of the bronze be made. Christie, unfamiliar with the stallion, was still skeptical.

"I just wondered to myself, who else would want to buy this bronze? I knew Duane would buy one and they were giving one to the Jensens but that only accounted for two of them! But, I didn't want to dampen their spirits so I told Duane that before I went to work on the project, I needed $1,000 down from 10 people and it would be non-refundable. He said okay. I really thought that would be the end of it, but in less than 15 minutes he called back and said, 'I've sold 11 of them. When can you start?' "

Christie, completely astounded by the response to the project, agreed to get started right away.

"I'll never forget when I went to do the sketches and measurements," stated Christie. "Charlie Ward and I jumped in a truck and drove out to this pasture and I'm looking all over the pasture for a famous stallion! I see this horse off in the distance, but I thought to myself, no, that can't be him; there are mares that are bigger than he is in this pasture, but Charlie drove right up to him."

Doc Bar proved to a cooperative gentleman while the somewhat long ordeal of being measured and photographed from every angle took place. Christie measured, sketched and handled the stallion, who patiently waited, somewhat unconcerned with the necessities of sculpting homework. When the session ended, Christie was surprised when another Doc Bar personality surfaced.

"He was quite comical. He had stood so still and quiet while I was doing all of this and then, when Charlie let him go, off he ran bucking and kicking like a snorty old bronc!"

To Christie's surprise, the bronze proved to be such a success that in less than a week of the first order, the number of editions that had been planned, already needed increasing. After finishing the sculpture and before casting it, the artist had it approved by Pacific Coast Quarter Horse Association. Nevertheless, when the bronze was finally finished, one particular purchaser doubted the authenticity of it.

"The night of the presentation, one of the directors got me aside and said he was going to sell the bronze he had purchased because Doc Bar's nose was too straight," said Christie. "He also thought I had a couple of flaws, like a place on his shoulder and a bad mark on his leg."

Christie suggested to the bronze owner that before he offered his bronze for sale, he might want to take a good look at the stallion, because Doc Bar did indeed have a straight nose, as well as a scar on his shoulder and hip. Since the stallion was coming to the presentation, Christie asked the owner to use the opportunity to look at the horse."

"He found me later that night and said, "you know, you're absolutely right!"

## Honoring Doc Bar:

As soon as he finished his lunch, Charlie Ward strolled to the barn to groom Doc Bar for his presentation that evening at the San Francisco Cow Palace. Although Doc Bar was 25 years old, the Wards had been asked to bring the stallion to a special ceremony honoring him during the Grand National Horse Show. Years of caring for horses made Charlie a pro at the chore and in only a short while, Doc Bar, whiskers trimmed, hair coat brushed and hooves polished, gleamed like a show horses. As soon as Stephenie was ready, he loaded Doc Bar in the trailer and the two hauled their life-long friend to San Francisco.

Charlie had barely pulled onto the coliseum parking lot and opened the trailer door to unload the horse when Doc Bar fans surrounded the trailer, straining for a glance of the famous stallion.

"When we arrived, we were surprised there were so many people there to see him unloaded," stated Stephenie. "We just didn't realize the magnitude of the event; we thought we were bringing him in for a little ceremony."

Since there were still several hours before the presentation began, Charlie took Doc Bar to his assigned stall. It was specially decorated with plants and his name was proudly displayed across its front. The crowds immediately encircled it.

"There was a mob of people all around his stall," remembered Stephenie, "standing, looking, delighted to see him. He had been out of the public eye for so long and since those years when he was being shown, a lot of new people had gotten into the horse business. They had never seen him."

It was an evening to remember. The stallion, still a showman, played to the excited crowd as Charlie took him around the arena. Despite his age and the numerous years away from the spotlight, the showmanship in him returned.

**Doc Bar being honored at the Cow Palace.**

This photo of Doc Bar's head was taken by Christie for his sculpture. Note that Doc Bar does not have an Arabian dish in his nose like some people thought he had.

It was as if he was looking for a photographer!" laughed Christie.

"He came alive," remembered Darryl Chapman, head of the Cow Palace Livestock Center. It was something that everybody talked about. His nostrils flared and he pranced into the arena as if a young stallion."

"People just wouldn't stop clapping," remembered Sue Hearst. "It was such a thrill. I felt like I was in the presence of something special."

And it was also the last time that the stallion would be displayed to the public. "We loaded him up and took him back home that night after the presentation," said Stephenie, " and the entire next day he laid down. He was just so tired.

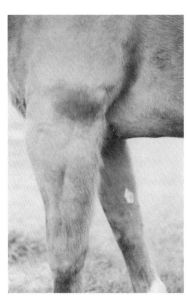

This photo of Doc Bar's left front leg, taken by Keith Christie for his sculpture, showed a scar, which ultimately ended up on the sculpture.

The trip had taken a lot out of him. Charlie decided then that Doc Bar had left the ranch for the last time. After that, we had a lot of offers to take him out, but Charlie said, "no."

## Other Awards:

Doc Bar had also been presented at the Cow Palace when the presentation awards were first introduced by the Pacific Coast Quarter Horse Association. At that time, Charlie attested to the stallion's cutting ability.

"I was legging him up, getting him ready to go. I'd saddle him in the evenings after I had worked my other horses and ride him down to the river to let the cattle out. That's when I drove a cow around on him a little bit for my own benefit. He certainly had cow in him. He had just gotten so valuable though that we couldn't afford to haul him around to shows. Besides, by then his get were proving him.

The California Reined Cow Horse Association also honored the stallion with their famous plaques. The one hanging in the Ward home reads, "When we hung up their bridles, we took off our hats to honor Doc Bar." The award was in honor of the legacy that the great stallion had left on the California reined cow horse.

And finally, in May, 1993, almost a year after his death, Doc Bar, one of the most influential sires in the American Quarter Horse breed was inducted into the American Quarter Horse Hall of Fame during the 1993 American Quarter Horse Association Convention.

# 17

## *The End*

*To every thing there is a season, and a time to every purpose under the heaven; A time to be born, and a time to die, a time to plant, and a time to pluck up that which is planted; a time to kill, and a time to heal; a time to break down, and a time to build up; a time to weep, and a time to laugh, a time to mourn and a time to dance...a time to get and a time to lose; a time to keep and a time to cast away.*
       *Ecclesiasties 3: 1-6*

*&#42;&#42;&#42;*

"Gee, I'm glad you're here close by so you can take care of some things when it's time, " commented Charlie Ward as he shook hands with his new neighbor, Darryl Lund. Lund, a plumber by trade and a horseman by heart, had been a member of the Pacific Coast Quarter Horses Association for more than a quarter of a century, so he and the Wards had been acquaintances for many years. Now he had moved to the valley, and lived only miles down the road from them.

Lund's nod of his head assured Charlie that Lund knew the thought behind his unspoken words. Doc Bar, although really faring well for a horse in his 30's, had the normal physical ailments of age which were naturally taking their toll.

Frequently, Charlie and Stephenie mentioned how fortunate they were that he had lived so long since few horses lived into their 30's. They often talked around the subject of his death but the thought of putting Doc Bar down rarely surfaced into words, just as it had not done with Lund. Charley, though, knew that day was rapidly approaching and someone with Lund's expertise and heavy equipment would be necessary then. It would be nice to have him close by.

The leaves on the side of the mountains sported colors of orange, yellow and gold when Darryl's telephone rang one day. Charlie, on the other end of the line, just wanted him to know that Doc Bar wasn't doing well and he wanted to make sure Lund would be around for the next couple of days.

Lund, however, in the days ahead never received that expected phone call. Instead, the stallion, which, until that time had never been ill a day in his life, improved remarkably and all thoughts of euthanasia vanished.

Winter rolled into spring. Stephenie, while planting flowers in the yard, gazed at her old friend standing very still in a nearby pen. Last night she had suggested to Charlie that maybe it was time, but he had said, "No, not yet."

She understood. It had only been weeks earlier when winter blasts plummeted their valley and while she rubbed Doc Bar down in the barn, Charlie made the suggestion to her that perhaps it was time. Then, almost angrily, she had stated adamantly, 'no, not yet', and rubbed all the harder to stimulate his circulation.

"One would decide it was time to put him down," remembered Lund, "and the other one couldn't agree. It was a tough decision, one that they agonized over for more than a year."

Doc Bar was more than just a horse to Charlie and Stephenie Ward. He had been a part of their lives for 30 years, so much a part that Stephenie's folks, when incorporating, changed the name of the ranch from Double J to Doc Bar.

Daily, for the past 23 of those years, the couple had brushed, bred, petted and fed him. Why, he had stayed with them longer than their children! They had laughed at his whimsical ways of posing, smiled at his soldier-like answer to the duty of breeding, and felt pride as he proved himself to the world from the valley of California. Their passions for Doc Bar ran deep.

Lund watched while his friends, realizing each marching hour brought closer the day of the decision to put him down, tried time and again to come to terms with the inevitable. Doc Bar, 36 years old, had just been around for so long. The Pony Express, itself, only lasted one year, the 18th amendment on prohibition had a young life of 4 years; even the Futurities which he had so heavily influenced, weren't as old as he was. Saying goodbye, especially when you made the decision when to do it, was difficult.

Worse, though, would be to allow the great stallion to agonize with every movement and to strain to the point of exertion for only a morsel of food. No, they would not allow that. Helping others sometimes meant hurting oneself.

In early July, Charlie and Stephenie finally agreed it was time, perhaps after the Salinas rodeo. Charlie feared the horse might get down sometime when he was away from the ranch and be unable to get up. Doc Bar had grown thinner and thinner since during the last few months, his intestines had stopped absorbing nutrients. Charlie mentioned it to Lund.

"I had been involved in things like that before," said Lund. "I've buried some really good horses through the years. It's really hard on all of us, but especially for the owners.

"I was at the rodeo showing my horse and talked to the vet, Dr. Deter, about coming out to my ranch for some vet work Monday morning. We mentioned Doc Bar. We all knew it was time to put him down, so I waited until Sunday evening and called Charlie.

"Charlie, I'm coming out tomorrow morning. You know, Gary is coming too."

"Oh, well, yeah, it's time."

It was over within an hour. By 8:00 a.m. Monday morning, Lund had already dug a hole with a ramp behind the home of Charlie and Stephenie, the place they wanted their friend buried. Shortly thereafter, the distant hum of an arriving airplane signaled Dr. Gary Deter's arrival.

Stephenie left. As the men set about the business of ending an era, she walked the road. And cried. And walked some more.

"I still was out at the ranch frequently for one thing or another, but for some reason I had not been there in about a month," said Dr. Deter, " so I was really surprised when I saw how rapidly Doc Bar had declined in such a short period of time. Up until then he had stayed so good and muscular for his age, but when I saw him that day, I couldn't believe how he had changed. All of a sudden he was old."

Doc Bar stood quietly in his stall as Charlie walked alone to the barn to retrieve the stallion one last time. He had made this same walks so many times for so many years. Before, Charlie had been taking him to give life; this time he was taking him to be relieved of one that had lost its luster, that had nothing left but pain and discomfort.

Without a word, Charlie placed the halter around Doc Bar's neck, then led him slowly out into the bright sunshine. June 20, 1992, Charlie thought to himself as he walked Doc Bar down the ramp and into the hole where Gary Deter waited. He'd never forget this day.

Turning Doc Bar around, Charlie took off the halter, giving his old friend one last pat as Deter quickly administered the shot.

It was a beautiful day. Summer crinkled in the air while a slight, billowy breeze stirred the sky. The three men, all with moist eyes, said nothing. A deep sadness, although cushioned by the beautiful morning, nudged away the burden of indecision that had rested for so long on Charlie's shoulders. The sadness settled itself in its place. Stephenie continued to walk.

Finally, Gary Deter and Charlie, with Doc Bar's halter hanging on his arm, walked away while Lund buried Doc Bar.

It was time to call Dr. Jensen.

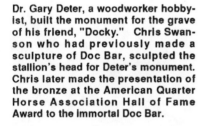

Dr. Gary Deter, a woodworker hobbyist, built the monument for the grave of his friend, "Docky." Chris Swanson who had previously made a sculpture of Doc Bar, sculpted the stallion's head for Deter's monument. Chris later made the presentation of the bronze at the American Quarter Horse Association Hall of Fame Award to the immortal Doc Bar.

# Other Works by Gala Nettles

| | |
|---|---|
| Just Shorty | $19.95 |
| Mr. Pat | $19.95 |
| Cutting Capers | $ 9.95 |
| Training The Horse And Rider | $29.95 |

All books can be purchased by calling 1-800-729-2234 or writing LMH Publishing Company, Route 2, Box 60, Groesbeck, Texas 77864.